DISCOVERING TWINS

A JOURNEY INTO LIVES

STELLA TER HART

IngramSpark

PRAISE FOR DISCOVERING TWINS

Emotionally charged and beautifully written
... a page-turner.

After her mother's death, Stella begins to look into her family history, unaware of the tragic story she is about to unearth. She examines the matters of racism, hate and violence against humanity, cruelty, and questions of faith and identity with precision and skill. A riveting and often brutal tale of the horrors of the Holocaust with family and relationships at its core, this is a winner."

— THE PRAIRIES BOOK REVIEWS

DISCOVERING TWINS

An innocent comment about the tradition of twins in the family from her mother during her pregnancy leaves ter Hart wondering about her family's history. Deeply profound and achingly beautiful, the book aptly explores innate yearning for one's roots while delving into the horrors of war and genocide, familial bonds, love, loss, and grief.

This is a stunner.

— BOOKVIEW REVIEWS

This work contains both fiction and non-fiction. All characters presented are either based on, or are, actual individuals. Although this work does not purport to be an historical treatise, it can be used for learning and educational purposes, particularly to those exposed to these events for the first time.

ISBN : 978-1-7775108-0-0

For my cousin, Samuel, for bringing me into his present and sharing his own journey into our family's past.

For my mother, who struggled with her secrets but still brought me in to some of them.

For my uncle, Giovanni (Joe) Vittali, and cousin, Johannes Vittali, who both gave me stories from their perspective of the family that I would otherwise have never known.

For my family —past, present, and future, near and far —this story is a part of all of us.

Ignorance is the root and stem of all evil.

Plato
(circa 428 — 348 BCE)

What you leave behind is not what is engraved in stone monuments, but what is woven into the lives of others.

Pericles
(circa 495-429 BCE)

CONTENTS

PROLOGUE

This is a true story. It is the story of family, the discovering of family, and the discovery of secrets, hidden, but hoping desperately to be found. The names, places, and events are real. The dates are real.

Scattered amongst the many memories are stories where the only truths available were gleaned from fragmented bits of information and genealogical sets of dates. I imagined my way through these bits to create glimpses into lives unknown.

These stories, though fictionalized, are historically accurate for their time. Much of the detail described— even the tiniest details of items, possessions, food, phrases and places—mirrors my own life experiences, or is based on stories shared amongst relatives. Historical events alluded to or directly referenced are the result of intensive internet research spurred on by the briefest of dates.

To add a bit of linguistic texture, various Dutch words and phrases I grew up with are sprinkled throughout this manuscript. The meanings are transparent enough to be understood, but for those needing guidance, a translations list can be found at the end of the book.

I quote a myriad of dates, which at first give the impression of a rather long list of tedious numbers and data. Most writers avoid dates like the plague! But this story exists almost exclusively *because* of the dates. A deeper reflection of them reveals truths so dark the mind flounders to navigate through them.

This is not a Holocaust story per se, and yet, the Holocaust looms. There are no brilliant escapes, no miraculous heroic feats. The viewpoints narrow in on life before that time, at that time—then interrupted for all time.

Crucial past experiences and events, never fully understood before but now imbued with a clearer understanding, are woven around this journey into lives, transforming details into reality.

Although the tragedies presented are heart wrenching, the fact that I am here to share them, and able to preserve those shared with me, gives them a new, almost victorious life. Their uncovering strengthens that indomitable human instinct to claim and protect what is ours, even after it has been stolen away.

~

*Sophia Maria Vittali-ter Hart and daughter,
Stella ter Hart. Estevan, Saskatchewan,
circa 1961.*

1982 - CALGARY

EXPECTING

"*T*wins run in the family, you know," said my mother. A surprising statement with no introduction or precedent. A comment as benign as stating hazel eyes or curly hair ran in the family. And no, I didn't know.

It was the summer of 1982. I was expecting my first child. Pregnancy being all-consuming, the unexpected maternal remark of the moment felt appropriate, despite its interjection.

My mind wandered to the first twins in my life — one a friend of my brothers — half of a set of fraternal twins. I had no clue. When I met him with his sister for the first time, I couldn't decipher what was in front of me — two faces, identical to a degree, but one male, one female. How do you explain that?

Complex baby biology was beyond my stage of awareness in 1974 at age fourteen. Forget internalizing the concept of two humans developing from two distinct eggs, or the spontaneous division of the same egg. An introverted girl growing up in the isolated prairie town of

Estevan, Saskatchewan, nine miles north of the North Dakota border, its pioneer and immigrant population 9,102, I was at best, naïve, and at worst, uneducated.

Penny and Paul. The memory of them pops in my mind. Brother and sister with shared, long oval-shaped faces, copious freckles, and straight brown hair glinting red in the sun.

Dominated by two older brothers and eclipsed by a much younger sister, I wished I had a twin.

You would think, once past the shock, a multiple birth would be highly efficient and practical. One pregnancy, two children. Instant family. I prided myself on being the epitome of efficiency, with my enthusiastic economizing and keen eagerness to accomplish as much as humanly possible in the shortest amount of time. A favourite challenge—fill a cart of groceries via coupons and *buy 1 get 1 free* specials. Come to think of it, twins would be rather like that—*buy 1 get 1 free.*

Economy and thriftiness were habits absorbed from my parents, necessary survival techniques forced upon them as teenagers in Holland during World War II. Thrift became their shared lifetime mantra: save where you could, use what you had, then do without, the habits continueing long after such necessity lost its urgency. Perhaps thriftiness is one of those rare positives gleaned by surviving a war, any war, anywhere, anytime.

We had no other family in Canada. My parents married in Europe, then immigrated in the late 1950s. My father's family—elderly parents and one younger sister— remained in Holland while my mother's family—parents, older sister, older brother and younger brother—almost without notice, shipped themselves and their entire household off to Australia in 1947. My mother stayed behind in Amsterdam to pursue a career in the Dutch government.

Growing up, relatives separated by such vast distances meant zero opportunity to develop meaningful relationships with those so far away. Yet these absent family members occupied a crucial part of my psyche. A childhood devoid of relatives within reach makes those out of reach extra precious. I assumed these genetically connected people were all the family that existed beyond ourselves.

As far as elusive family twins went, this was news to me, despite my mother's dropped comment. Strange that there had been no mention of them before, where they were, or who they were attached to. But this fresh information didn't stick with me, my only concern being that of my own present.

What an innocent daydream, to delight in the conception of twins. These duplicated humans fascinate us, capturing our imagination with their intangible magic. Whose eye isn't drawn to those double strollers with double babies oft-times sharing a single face?

Sadly, in 1982, I wasn't having them.

EXPANSION

"*Schoontje, Schoontje, waar ben jij?*" Israel Wijnschenk leapt up the steep, worn wooden stairs to their third-storey canal house two narrow steps at a time. "I've got fabulous news!"

"*Hou op*, not so loud!" Brows furrowed, a lined but still lovely face poked out from around a heavy front door. Iron hand-wrought hinges creaked in protest at the onslaught of disturbing, pounding thuds headed their way. With a sigh, Schoontje Wijnschenk tucked an escaped lock of wavy blonde hair back under her kerchief. "You'll wake the baby! *Oma's* only now put him down."

"Ah, there you are, my beautiful one," Israel flashed a mischievous grin as his wife glared at him from the landing outside their tiny three-room upper apartment. With a few teasing love pats on her massively pregnant belly, and a wide, lunging step around her, he pulled the door wide open. Two bright-faced children spilled through and clambered around him.

"Papa! Papa! Papa!" Chubby little hands pulled at

his legs and grabbed his knees, reaching up for attention. Their father, a short man, but stocky and muscular from long days working in the Amsterdam shipyards, reached down and nabbed both children at once, swinging one onto his back and hoisting another under his arm.

Squeals of delight filled the air in the little Dutch home with its delicate handmade lace curtains discreetly covering draughty windows, and demure crocheted doilies protecting precious wood surfaces, obsessively dusted.

Massive oak beams crisscrossed a crumbling plaster ceiling punctuated with polished copper pots hanging from black cast-iron hooks. Above the mantel, dozens of ancient Delft tiles, patterned together with careful skill, formed a fresco of birds and flowers, their blue and white crispness brightening the otherwise dark room.

A mainstay of every Dutch home—an elaborate, oak grandfather clock—stood watch over the family from its vantage point against a white-washed plaster wall. Atlas, in hammered brass, stood atop, shoulders bent under the weight of the world. Scenes of Dutch life, also fashioned from brass, formed a border around the Titan, while the clock's tile face quietly swept over a scene of ships, windmills, and wind-blown clouds. The eternal *tick tock, tick tock* a comfort in times of peace and an irritant in times of stress.

Schoontje's mother, Anna, widowed and living with her only daughter, emerged in a huff from the kitchen. In a puff of white she abruptly dusted floured hands on her embroidered apron, scorch holes from decades of stirring over burning cook stoves pinpointing its worn surface.

"Where is your sense? *Ben je helemaal gek?*" Glaring at her son-in-law, she gesticulated a gnarled finger towards a toddler sleeping in the hand-crafted cradle warming beside the hearth.

"Ah, *lieve schoonmoeder*." Israel turned towards his mother-in-law. "Now, at last, I have something to make you proud!" He flashed another grin. "The supervisor spoke with me in private today. I'm to be promoted to a new position in the yard, and ..." Israel paused. His eyes darting playfully from one woman to the next, enjoying their instant looks of annoyance at his stopping mid-sentence. "One with more money!"

He deposited the two wriggling children back onto the floor, grabbed Anna's calloused hand and twirled her around before she could utter another word. "And who can complain about more money?"

"Will we be able to move to a bigger house?" Schoontje busied herself setting their small table for supper, manoeuvring her unwieldy bulk around inanimate household obstacles with surprising agility. An irresistible aroma from the steaming pot of soup on the fire wafted through the room that served as kitchen, eating area, sitting room, and her mother's living quarters.

Schoontje had always wanted a bustling family. The only child of her parents, she dreamed of a house full of babies; her own home, one brimming with laughter and love. If children were a blessing to a married couple, then Israel and Schoontje Wijnschenk were blessed indeed—seven now and another due in a month. Strange how healthy and full of life she felt when when she was pregnant, and how oddly empty and unfulfilled she felt when she was not.

But this pregnancy was not like any of her others. There was so much pain and swelling in her legs and so much pressure on her pelvis. She was huge. Was it her age? And the kicking! It was never-ending. When the kicking stopped, the rolling began—day in and day out. Leaving the house was awkward to the point of embarrassment, her need to urinate overcoming her at the most inconvenient times.

At the market, while picking out the day's vegetables or a filet of fresh fish, her eye would catch old housewives garnering that certain knowing look, nodding to her with toothless smiles, *"Er is meer dan een kleine Hansje in die kelder."*

"We have all we need right here." Head down, breathing in its savour, Israel dipped a dark, thick slice of crusty rye bread into his equally thick green pea soup. "Everyone we love is here. We fit in here. People are the same as us here."

Five children under twelve, little wooden bowls in hand, either stood or sat on the floor, slurping down their supper with hungry contentment. Tucked into the corner was a well-worn mahogany drop-leaf table reserved only for the adults, with the two eldest children, Salomon and Betje, counted among them.

Schoontje fixed a firm yet calm gaze on her husband. "Yes, I know, but there is no longer room for us, and the baby will be here soon." Her voice took on a deeper, more suggestive tone. "The girls are getting older. They can no longer share a room with all these boys."

Israel paused the delicious in-depth conversation he was enjoying with his soup and took in Schoontje's determined face. "All right, my beautiful one, all right. I promise to ask around if any of the men hear of a bigger place available. Something in *het oude Markenpleintje* perhaps."

Mother and daughter exchanged satisfied glances. They carried on helping the young ones finish their dinner. Afterwards, all were scrubbed up, changed into woollen nightclothes, and headed off to bed. The children doubled up in bunk beds in one room; eldest on the bottoms and littlest ones on top.

The next morning the sun rose unseen, shrouded behind a grey veil covering a dull North Sea sky. Heavy June air hugged the ground in a cold, damp fog. The working men of Amsterdam—young, old, strong, weak—had long since trudged off to factories and shops, swooshed out the door by busy mothers and bossy wives.

"Koopman!" Poking her head out the window into the drizzly day, Schoontje called to her second son, a tall, athletic boy playing stickball on the street below. "Run to the shipyards. Fetch your father and brother!" His mother's voice carried a tone that left no room for questioning, so without a word, the wiry eight-year-old abandoned his friends and ran to collect his father.

Now that he was sixteen, Solomon, the eldest Wijnschenk son, worked alongside his father and was proud to contribute to the family. Determined to prove himself and master new tasks, he worked as hard as any man in the yard, and was gaining a reputation for his natural ship-building skills.

He was also old enough to understand the urgency of his younger brother's instruction and sudden interruption into their workday. Salomon considered himself a man. Eavesdropping on multiple conversations between his father and uncles had opened his eyes about life.

The pains started mid-morning, unexpectedly early. At thirty-nine, Schoontje was more than aware of the risks of giving birth again—a little late now. As she suddenly doubled over, the familiarity of it ripped through her, each stabbing contraction sending her reeling.

Anna, poised and ready, was well-schooled in childbirth, having delivered all of her daughter's previous babies. As the grandfather clock ticked obliviously on, Anna busied herself fluffing pillows and organizing clean linens with bossy precision. She procured enormous supplies of boiling wash-water and much needed fresh, cold water. But now it was time.

"Betje. *Kijk eventjes!*" Startled, the eldest daughter glanced up from where she was sitting by an open window, obliviously daydreaming, an unread book lying open in her lap. Her Oma, arms loaded with a mountain of folded towels, stood large in front of her, tiny beads of sweat dampening her thinning, grey hair. At fourteen, Betje was considered a woman, and, terrified that her grandmother was expecting her to assist at the birth, had quietly retreated to the children's bedroom.

"Take your brothers and sister over to Tante Klaartje's. Stay there until someone comes to fetch you. It may be awhile, so bring along everyone's nightclothes."

When her sister, Rachel, was born, Betje was only eight, and at home. The terrifying sights and sounds of birthing were not an experience she wanted to relive. With an enormous sigh of relief, she began scurrying about the house rounding up her siblings, then herded them up the two blocks to Tante Klaartje's.

Her aunt, the youngest sibling on her father's side, was a heavenly vision of pure delight. She greeted everyone with a sweet, welcoming smile made ever the more beautiful by her dark, almond-shaped, softly expressive eyes. To Betje, Tante Klaartje displayed the embodiment of perfection, the feminine ideal, and instilled hope in her that she, too, could grow up to be so admired. Everyone did say she had her aunt's eyes!

She could rely on Tante Klaartje to have platefuls of

treats, enough to appease the coming onslaught of visiting cousins plus her own little one. Such temptations were guaranteed to keep Betje's pesky brothers quiet, at least as long as the *koekjes* held out.

Father and sons hurried back from the shipyard. Worried and terse, no words passed between them. Men did not speak of the birthing of children—that event which they found themselves shifted to the outside, floundering. The beginning of the creation of new life was more to their liking than the end result of it.

Her face rigid and stoic, Anna battled hiding feelings of worry and dread for her daughter. Childbirth had not been easy for Schoontje, despite her stoic nature and determined desire for a large family. The memory of a tiny little son—stillborn after a long, suffering labour drawn out over two days—a memory still raw and biting. Quickly following the one lost, another baby boy, healthy, and now a bubbling three-and-a-half-year-old. But more sorrow, as the next child, yet another boy, lived only a few short weeks. Anna paused in her busyness to wonder at the indomitable inner strength, iron will, and remarkable resiliency of women.

As if connected in thought to her mother, Schoontje too found herself comparing this present labour to her last—one almost effortless, a welcome surprise. Such a beautiful child, born perfect in every way. Had he been a gift from God to replace her baby born dead? When newborn little Abraham died two-and-a-half weeks later, Schoontje was inconsolable.

And now, fifteen months past, here she was staring at the same possibility again. Every woman, when her time is upon her, feels the grip of Death and prays for release as she suffers bringing new life into the world.

Though drained by the long hours of labour,

Schoontje still insisted on standing, leaning her full weight against Israel, for the worst of the contractions. If only his body could absorb her pain. Schoontje's piercing agony brought tears to his eyes.

After the death of her last infant son, Schoontje became obsessed with having more children. Girls. She wanted girls! Israel worked to persuade her that they had enough children—their family was complete. Labour was too hard on her, the suffering too much. But nothing he said could change her mind.

"Children are our key to immortality." Schoontje loved philosophizing over cups of strong coffee—sugared, hot, and topped with fresh cream. Israel always hand-ground the fragrant beans in advance in the *koffiemolen*, ready for a lazy Saturday and its welcome Sabbath rest from all work.

"After we are gone, they continue, and if you think about it, we are never really gone, as children carry in themselves all of who we are." Schoontje paused for a moment, her gentle, wondering eyes drawn to their small kitchen window. Beneath it lay Amsterdam, its inhabitants carrying on with life as they had for hundreds of years: a *kleine meisje* selling flowers, the baker with his bread cart, fishmongers, milk wagons, and old men with pipes, puffing, sitting silent, watching. But theirs was a changing world in 1840. Britain dominated the new steam engine industry, while Germany and France's unheard of outputs of iron signalled a revolution to a new and prosperous modern era.

"Just imagine—100 years from now—with all the innovation and change in the world, our descendants will undoubtedly enjoy a much better life than what we have today. Perhaps some may even move to America!"

Powerful contractions overtook her with unrelenting

frequency, each one more crushing than the last. Schoontje hung on Israel, clutching his arm with such ferocity his teeth clenched as her nails dug into his flesh. From some primal instinct buried deep within came a nonhuman, uncontrollable sound.

"It's coming! I feel it! I have to push!" she groaned. Holding his wife's full weight, Israel helped her squat above the pillows and pile of clean linens her mother had arranged on the floor. With a ferocious push, accompanied by unintelligible guttural inflections, Schoontje felt the baby slide out of her.

Towel-covered maternal hands, patient and waiting, caught this new grandson, tiny but healthy, whole, and blessed with an operatic set of lungs. Israel reached out as Anna passed him his child—a minuscule infant, cradled in one palm.

Israel's rough, powerful hands, accustomed to handling massive rigging, washed and swaddled the child with a quiet, natural gentleness. Carefully, he laid the baby in the new wooden cradle built to celebrate this one's arrival. Only the sturdiest oak had been sourced for its construction, and many a long, candlelit evening had been spent on its creation. Designed with elaborate inlays and crafted with balance and precision, it was destined to shelter many babies in its future.

Exhausted and weakened, Schoontje, with Anna grasping her on one side and Israel balancing the other, awkwardly pulled herself up off the floor. But her attempt to settle comfortably into bed resulted in writhing pain. Her eyes flashed with fear as new, startling waves of contractions overtook her.

"Something's wrong!" Staring down at her belly, its size protruding up from under the bedcovers like a pile of potatoes, realization struck that she was almost as pregnant now as before.

A hard kick. Then another—in a different place altogether! With a resigned drop, her head fell back on the feather pillows. She still had babies inside her. But how many? God give her the strength to endure the bringing of them into the world.

Two days later, Anna's face, worn but shining with love, beamed down at the three tiny infants asleep in the cradle where only one had been expected. First a boy, then a girl followed by another boy. After almost four days of labour it was a miracle that mother and babies all survived.

"There have been twins in our family in the past as I recall," Anna reflected aloud, remembering, "but triplets? A blessing times three."

From across the room came the clear voice of her daughter evincing pure contentment, "You could most definitely say that I now have that large family of my dreams."

1978 - ESTEVAN

THE JOURNEY

*M*y mother surprised me with a high school graduation gift of a month-long trip to Holland. Innocent at the outset, that trip would prove to be life-changing, not, as one might think, from eye-opening cultural experiences or visiting stunning, ancient architecture, but by the gradual revealing of unspeakable truths, long hidden.

July 5, 1978. Our journey encompassed a two-hour car drive from my hometown of Estevan, Saskatchewan, to Regina, Saskatchewan, followed by a four-hour Air Canada flight from Regina to Toronto, an eight-hour stopover in Toronto, then, finally, an eight-hour non-stop KLM flight from Toronto to Amsterdam. Although eighteen years old, I had never flown commercially before.

My previous aviation experience comprised one lone flight in a Cessna 150 piloted by my eldest brother, Jan, a few years earlier. At the conclusion of half an hour of my brother showing off his acrobatic aviation skills, the plane's sudden turns and downward swoops resulted in a lost lunch upon landing as I exited via a mad dash out the side of the plane.

Air Canada refrained from such manoeuvres, to my great relief. On our KLM flight, the unexpected constant supply of onboard meals, drinks, and snacks surprised and spoiled my happy, unabashed self—no need to open the package of Ritz crackers I had smuggled into my purse.

Zulma, my father's younger sister, and her husband, Theo, greeted us at the Schiphol Airport. Off we drove in what seemed a toy dinky car compared to the wood-trimmed Ford Country Squire eight-seater family station wagon back home.

Our route took us through the modern section of Amsterdam, then away from the centuries-old harbour, out of the city, and into the picturesque village of Heemstede. My aunt and uncle lived in a charming three-storey brick house, #6 Crayenestersingel, directly opposite a gently flowing canal.

WHEN I WAS FIVE, *Tante* Zulma, *Oom* Theo and my cousins, Dirk Jan and Tessa, visited Canada. Any details of their two-month stay I can only recall through old photographs—I have no direct memory of it.

Six-year-old Dirk Jan arrived speaking zero English and left fluent, a gift imposed upon him by my older brothers, Jan and Bert, who spoke precious little Dutch. Dirk Jan, outnumbered two to one in the playmate category, had no choice but to learn to speak to these strange cousins at their level, in their language, and in real time.

Years later, Dirk Jan mentioned this memorable

vacation in Canada, and how learning English during that summer of 1965 catapulted him forward in his education and indeed, his life.

~

MY *OPA* RESIDED AT A SENIORS' home not from his daughter, Zulma. He and *Oma* had retired at age sixty-three and moved there, the thought of burdening their daughter by moving in with her unthinkable. The Dutch are nothing if not practical. Opa, at the time of my Holland trip in 1978, was eighty-nine and long widowed. I had met him only once before in 1969 when he came to stay with us for four months.

A delightful, almond-eyed, long-lashed child, I spent my days singing and dancing for no-one in particular, curling dandelion stems, catching butterflies, and generally smiling and flitting about. Opa, however, preferred quieter children. "Why can't you be more like your friend, Shelley?" He scowled at me one day from the kitchen sink while washing the dishes. He washed dishes constantly—his way of contributing to the household.

Instant silence. Instant sadness. A crushing moment of realization that your grandfather—this mysterious, far-away relative, the patriarchal embodiment of your entire family whom you had never encountered before—didn't seem to like you, and wished you were someone else.

His wild and free Canadian grandchildren must have struck him as irresponsibly undisciplined, with their constant in and out of the house, roaming the neighbourhood at will and, apparently, singing and dancing out of context. In his day, children were *seen and not heard*.

That same summer, unaware of the *you dance too much*

comment, my mother enrolled me in the Reginald Hawe Ballet School in Regina, the capital city of Saskatchewan located a straight, flat as a run-over prairie gopher, car drive north-west. The camp was three weeks long—an interminable length of time smack dab in the middle of a coveted July.

Sophia Maria ter Hart-Vittali, my mother, faced many life challenges that year: juggling three children, ages nine, ten, and twelve, pleasing a stubborn, opinionated old father-in-law constantly underfoot, and all while seven months pregnant. At forty-one years old, this was probably not what she planned for her summer holiday.

A tiny attic bedroom was waiting for me in Regina at the grandmother's house of another girl from Estevan, also ballet school destined. Her name was Jan. Imagine my confusion at meeting a girl with the same name as my father and brother. Grandmothers existed akin to fairy godmothers in my mind: kind, generous, quiet, and patient, and most importantly, the queens of kitchens overflowing with homemade edible delights.

I never knew either of my grandmothers, and often imagined myself akin to the shivering orphan child in the fairy tale, *The Little Match Girl*—striking a blaze of light from a wooden bundle of matches, miraculously causing my grandmothers to appear. Taking pity on me in my loneliness, they would scoop me up in their arms and swoosh me off to a heavenly place.

My little room had one window overlooking a small, yet verdant backyard. Its curtain-less panes revealed a glorious view over the top of a magnanimous maple tree that shaded us from the scorching Saskatchewan summer sun. Underfoot—a wide-plank pine floor, soft, sun-worn, and faded from the passings of many feet. Overhead— slanted ceilings with generations of paint peeling off the plaster. Around—four walls, all the colour of an Alberta wild rose. Amidst all this old, proudly on display on the bedside table was a new radio—an enigma of shiny plastic, black with a silver antenna poking up.

Access to that radio produced in me a wonderfully grown-up feeling. I was never allowed to touch a radio at home; its presence was exhilarating and magical. The Beatles appeared to win the most airtime, and the song, *Nowhere Man*, in particular. My skinny, undeveloped body learned every word. I belted out the whole song at each airing!

As the radio poured out new music, the alternative world around me, so different from the one two hours southeast, introduced a strange sense of freedom. Over fifty years later, my mind slips back to the past every time an oldie graces the air waves.

One Saturday afternoon, Jan, my fellow ballerina-in-training, and I were dropped off at the Hudson's Bay store to spend a few carefree hours window-shopping and just wandering around. While leaving two girls alone in a large department store parent-free is unthinkable these days, it was perfectly acceptable in those simpler, safer times.

Didn't my eye catch a display of Silly Putty! If a nine-year-old can lust, I did, for Silly Putty! The price tag of $0.99 didn't daunt me. I devised a plan to get my silly little hands on some of that putty.

With eyelashes batting, I earnestly offered up assistance to my benevolent short-term landlady. For two weeks after classes, I pulled weeds, washed dishes, harvested lettuces, polished furniture, peeled potatoes and dusted doodads.

At the end of twenty-one days of toe pointing and arm poising, my mother drove up to Regina to retrieve me, and then it was back down to Estevan. Goodbye pink room of small delights. Hidden in my modest suitcase — ninety-nine pennies.

On an August afternoon, clutching my hard-earned wages, I journeyed the one-and-a-half miles on foot from Grundeen Crescent, Pleasantdale subdivision, to 4th Street, downtown Estevan. Destination: Green's Hardware Store. Mission: Silly Putty.

Mr. Green's store was legendary. Whatever you needed, he was guaranteed to have at least one. There was even a section of classical piano music and LP records off to the side near the rakes, hoes, shovels and seeds. I suppose one never knew when an avid gardener might hanker for a little Bach.

And he had toys! A terrific selection to tempt all ages. Mr. Green never seemed to care if neighbourhood kids stood and stared, picked and dropped, fingered and fondled. With a mild sense of panic, I scoured the shelves. Hot-Wheel cars, Spirographs, Barbie Dolls and Tonka Trucks. Then — there they were! I made a beeline and nabbed one of the egg-shaped packages containing my coveted prize from the selection of three varieties. I had my glow-in-the-dark Silly Putty! Feeling confident and quite grown-up, my one hand carefully placed its purchase onto the sales counter while the other simultaneously clinked ninety-nine copper pennies alongside, in complete obeisance to the price sticker.

"That will be one dollar and three cents," Mr. Green stated, busying himself with counting the pile of change on the counter. My eyes widened as tears welled up. I stared in despair. He was wrong! My experience in correcting adults was nil. "Excuse me, Mr. Green, but ..." He seemed eight feet tall while I wanted to shrink into the floor, "... but the sticker says ninety-nine cents."

"I'm so sorry, honey, but there's tax on that."

Confused, despondent, I gaped up at my Goliath. "What's tax?"

He stopped his counting to turn to look at me, his brows softening. His eyes smiled every so slightly with a gentle wrinkling, but his mouth was grim. "Never you mind," he said in a gentle voice. A look of inexorable sadness, regret, and pity overtook his face. "Ninety-nine cents is just fine."

Mr. Green watched, motionless, as the store bell jangled me out the front door, Silly Putty in hand. I've had issues with the fairness of taxes ever since.

While I was away at ballet camp, Opa had fallen off a ladder while changing a light bulb and broken his leg. He gave no indication of being happy to see me again. My parents—distracted and distant. Life seemed to have somehow shifted its mood. Perhaps it was an awakening awareness of what was always there—the daily strain and burden of adulthood.

ONE MORNING while on our Holland vacation, my mother and I decided to visit Opa at his Dutch retirement home. We arrived unannounced to interject, or so we hoped, an element of surprise into his otherwise monotonous days.

He welcomed us into his little room, a setting rich with family heirlooms, and centuries-old handmade solid oak furniture adorned with dusty photographs of people I did not recognize. 200-year-old Delft blue plates hung on the walls, gleaming silver candlesticks and a sterling tea set adorned his small, lace covered dining table.

Dapper in a formal black suit and tie, shoes polished

to perfection, and wearing a fedora, Opa escorted us down the hall and knocked on the door of his ninety-year-old lady-friend. Not expecting guests, she asked if we didn't mind waiting a moment or two for her to prepare herself. We stood obligingly outside her door. Soon she reappeared, all put-together, powdered, and stylishly dressed for the day, complete with silk stockings with seams up the back, circa 1940.

A grand piano graced the small stage in one of the larger meeting rooms. Opa asked if I would play something and qualified it with, "Are you any good?" Both his mother and grandmother had been amateur pianists. I climbed the four stairs to the stage, settled myself on the bench, and played Bach's *Prelude and Fugue #23 in B major* from Book 1 of *The Well-Tempered Clavier* — perfectly. At the last note, Jan ter Hart Senior got up without saying a word, and vacated the room. Unsure of what to do, I exited stage left and plunked myself down in the place where he had just been, seated beside my mother. In a redundant whisper, she leaned over and commented, "I thought it was pretty good?"

A few moments later my grandfather returned, this time with an entourage of equally exquisitely dressed elder friends! "Play something else."

Up I went again, and this time extended the spontaneous concert to include Debussy's *Arabesque #2 in A major*, the Kabalevsky *Variations*, Mozart's *Piano Sonata in Eb major*, and Chopin's *Nocturne in F minor*. I performed my way to redemption and absolved myself of any less shining opinions from earlier years. Opa had deemed my musical skills worthy of a wider audience. I restrained myself from indulging in any singing or dancing.

My mother had planned the agenda for our Holland trip months in advance, before I was even aware there was a plan. She loved being in charge, loved being the organizer and would never think to ask me for any input. But then, the only bits I knew about Holland came from my six-page Grade 4 history project, presented in the shape of a wooden shoe, so any input from me would have been rather thin.

As the children of strict European parents, we were not allowed to argue, disagree, or "talk back". Only once in my life did I stand up to my parents and challenge their response to a childish request. I begged to go to the movie, *The Boyfriend*, playing at the Orpheum Theatre in Estevan. Cheryl was going. Everyone was going.

My parent's combined answer? An unequivocal NO. But I fussed and whined, put on fake tears and pulled the "but Cheryl's parents are letting her go" ploy. Miraculously, NO changed to YES. What a shock! It was beyond comprehension that grown-ups could be so easily manipulated by a pouty pre-adolescent push-back. Victorious, off I went.

The movie was awful, and I felt equally awful about the behaviour that paid for my admission. It was beneath me, as if I had violated my own code of ethics by resorting to childhood terrorism. I never questioned, argued, or talked back to either of my parents ever again.

July in Holland, apart from its unexpected summer drizzle, so strange to one accustomed to a land of continuous July sun, was glorious. I experienced cheese market excursions, lavish flower gardens and a special day at the Rijks Museum where we were royally guided into a lower gallery for a private viewing of three paintings by the famous 19th century Dutch artist, Willem Maris.

My mother, before she was married and while working in Canberra, Australia, for the Dutch Embassy, serendipitously snapped up a Willem Maris painting of cows, a favourite theme of the artist, at a second-hand store for next to nothing. I remember where it hung in our living room when I was little; I would stand and gaze at it, imagining myself peeking out from behind the lone tree, hanging out with those calm and contented cows. It graces my living room now.

We took strolls past towering cathedrals, were sonorously transported into blissful worlds by heavenly organ concerts, attended *Wiener Blut* in style at the opera house clothed in our regal best, munched on elegant lunches of cheese, apple cake and tea at outside cafes, delighted in sliced sugared strawberries on white bread for breakfast, hand-fed pigeons in the Amsterdam town square, and marvelled at quaint thatched roofs rain-proofing old, old houses.

These were exquisite, unique experiences, but not unexpected. What *was* unexpected were the mysterious relatives who began to appear, one by one, two by two: great-aunts and great-uncles in great quantities. Mind-boggling. To go from believing our little family consisted of fewer than fifteen people to over fifty, all alive and well, created utter confusion in my impressionable mind. My not knowing much Dutch and they not speaking much English added to the fumbling awkwardness. I could barely straighten everyone out and attach them to each other according to their relationship to me.

One day two elderly *Tantes* (the Dutch word for aunts) came to tea at my Aunt Zulma's house on the Crayenestersingel. On the way in, one of my aunts stumbled on the front step. I, in an attempt to show empathy, and make a lasting first impression, let forth a Dutch expression, one my father might say.

Needless to say, since in his bachelor days Jan Daniel

ter Hart, the man who would become my father, had worked as an officer in the Dutch Merchant Navy, a life surrounded by only men for months at a time, his vocabulary was quite colourful.

My mother hurled me aside and hissed that I was never EVER to say, "that" word again. "Why? What did I say wrong? What did I do?" She couldn't even bring herself to explain the exact meaning behind the naively chosen expletive.

Only decades later, with the help of Google Translate, did I discover that, completely without intent and in total innocence, I called a dignified and elegant 88-year-old Dutch lady, a cunt. There's no polite way to cover that up. It's what I said. Extreme apologies to all.

Goal—create a lasting first impression, a scene never to be forgotten. Achieved? Undeniably! The only bonus? Parents aren't perfect; a life lesson best learned early on.

Language is a funny thing. A socially acceptable and perfectly ordinary word in one language can, in another language, be downright hilarious, scandalous, rude, or any number of things in-between.

My mother, while working at the Dutch Embassy in Ottawa, once paged her employer over the loudspeaker, "Mr. Rondvaart, telephone call. Paging Mr. Rondvaart, Mr. Rondvaart to the office please." All the other girls around her in the office were falling out of their chairs in hysterics. Sophia Vittali, in pure innocence, asked what was so funny. They gawked at her, mouths open, and fell into fits of giggles and laughter all over again.

Every day in Holland was dizzyingly wonderful. Instead of a hot, dusty prairie wind filling my lungs, there was cool, moist air perfumed with flowers. Instead of plastic wrapped Kraft processed cheese on my bread, my Dutch lunches boasted delicately sliced Gouda cheese, made in, literally, Gouda. Instead of needing to drive for hours in a hot, stuffy car to reach almost anywhere in the same province, we could walk to flourishing markets and cultural sites. Or, we could hop on a train, and in under fifteen minutes find ourselves in an entirely new part of the country.

I was content with my mother's clandestine agendas, with each new day promising an exciting, undiscovered mystery. Every street seemed to have some hidden meaning for her, the familiar places bringing back buried childhood memories: a favourite baker's stand now long gone, a flower seller's stall remembered, the local bookshop where you could still buy postcards, gifts, notebooks, and handmade stationary. Amsterdam was her old stomping ground, her home, her heritage. It was all fresh territory to me, so best to just tag along.

THE BIRTHDAY

*I*n exactly one month it would be Flora's tenth birthday. That meant, of course, that it would be her brother, Alexander's, as well. Twins with faces so much alike that people seeing them for the first time looked confused and, as if they thought she couldn't hear, would mutter, "Which one is the girl?"

Flora hated being so boyish, with her cropped black hair and skinny pin legs matching those of her brother's. Grimacing openly when her gender was in question, she didn't want to be ten. She wanted to be twenty-four, like her cousin, Femma. Femma was also a twin but tall, elegant, and strikingly beautiful with flawless olive skin and curvy figure. Beside her, Flora felt squat, flat, and ugly.

"Mama, are we going to have a party this year, me and Alexander?" She kept her eyes down, trying not to cut herself while helping her mother peel mounds of potatoes. Everything in her life was *we*, never the luxury of the individual *I*. "It's our tenth birthday, you know."

Regina van der Sluijs paused, tipped her head, and

smiled sideways at her youngest daughter, the last born of their family of five. "I've not forgotten." 1928. The year she and two of her cousins all had twins. Three sets in total within nine months of each another forming an endless parade of gargantuan swollen bellies from March through December.

"Would you like a party, *mijn lieve schatje*?" Straightening up from the bowl of earthy vegetables, Regina stretched backwards, strong hands on generous hips. At forty-seven, her body was betraying her, getting stiffer, moving slower. Everyday tasks took longer than in earlier years, with fewer children. "These extra pounds don't help," she thought, slowly easing her neck from side to side.

"Oh yes, we would love one! I'll even wear a dress, too, if you like." Flora's imagination sparked with images of fancy-wrapped presents, and all the delectable cakes her mother and numerous *Tantes* might bake.

"Well then, so shall it be!" The prospect of a noisy get-together to celebrate the miracle and joy of birthdays would be a much needed distraction from the gloomy negative news constantly rumouring throughout Holland these past few months. Everyone was so tense. "We can invite all the family."

ALL the family? Flora winced at the thought. So many relatives, all of them living practically underfoot, dropping in anytime they felt like it, handing over babies of all ages for her to entertain—and so many twins!

"Can Sophia come? She only lives fifteen minutes away." Her cousin, Sophia Vittali, was a year older. She didn't have a Jewish father like everyone else that Flora knew, but that didn't seem to matter. Family was family, and besides, Sophia was tons of fun! They often met at their Opa's house on weekends, and spent the afternoon together there. Sophia was allowed to ride the train to Opa Hijman's house on Saturdays instead of having to walk, like the other grandchildren. Flora didn't know why. This always made her feel left out, different, and a bit jealous.

"Of course she can, if it's all right with her parents." Giovanni Vittali had a reputation for a kind heart, a quick temper, a knack for business, but not much patience for children. Well-known for impeccable honesty and ethics, his building company was highly respected throughout Amsterdam. Betje Vittali, his wife, was quiet, gentle, loving, and benevolent.

The Vittali household regularly sat at dinner with unannounced visitors, spontaneously invited by Giovanni. An old widowed man today, a newly arrived stranger tomorrow. But Betje never complained, always ensuring every unfamiliar face felt at home at her table. Incredible how you can stretch out a meal by tossing in a few extra potatoes and an onion.

It caused quite the scandal, young Betje Hijman marrying a headstrong Italian, and was a devastating shock to her parents and grandparents. As the second eldest daughter in the family, genuine concern circulated in the Jewish community on whether it might tempt her younger brothers and sisters to follow suit.

But when baby Christina Elisabeth Vittali arrived a mere five months after the marriage, healthy and at an undeniably robust weight, any questioning of the "why" of the relationship stopped. None of that mattered anymore.

Yes, it would be wonderful to have Sophia. Her spontaneous laugh and bright nature would be a welcome addition to the festivities, not to mention providing much needed relief from noisy twin boys and their raucous behaviour!

And Duifje, yes, Duifje too. She was twelve, and the only girl in her small family of two children. Duifje lived even closer at an easy ten-minute walk. What a perfect idea. Three cousins, Flora, Sophia, and Duifje, giggling together and whispering secrets behind the backs of the boys, all the while stuffing themselves with cake.

"What about Klaartje and Greetje?" Flora babbled out another excited request. "They are the only other twin girls near our age and I never get to see them anymore!" Her mother's brows furrowed with the faintest trace of annoyance.

"I can ask, but don't get your hopes up." Regina abruptly turned her attention back to supper preparations. "Ever since they lost the baby, that family just hasn't been the same. They stick to themselves and don't want to see or talk to anyone."

Flora knew better than to poke the subject further. What does that even mean? *They lost the baby.* Where? Under the sofa? Left in the market or on the train? Adults could be so ridiculous. Just say it. *The baby died.*

"I'm not a child." Flora mumbled absentmindedly.

"What was that, *schatje*?"

"Oh nothing, Mama. I was just thinking about my birthday."

Regina set herself to planning an elaborative, festive menu. Word was sent to the family to come and share in the ten-year celebration of the birth of Alexander and Flora, the van der Sluis twins.

The One-Decade Birthday Day of Sunday, October 23, 1938, arrived. The cozy house at Vechtstraat 75 in Amsterdam was a flurry of preparations, delayed by the constant interruptions of enthusiastic family prematurely appearing on the doorstep.

Boisterous exclamations, greetings, and congratulations flooded around the twins. "Flora, look at you! Have you grown?" Tante Helena eyed her up and down, talking incessantly. "You're absolutely adorable in that pink dress. Did your mother sew it for you? However did she find the time? Those puffed sleeves are so stylish! Finally, *moeder's mooiste,* you look like a girl." Alexander stuck his tongue out at his sister as she turned from the flood of comments to hide her dislike of them.

"When are you going to grow your hair longer? You really must let it grow. Why do you keep it so short?" She turned back around and there was Femma, her idol, looking down at her with those captivating eyes. "You have such lovely hair. So curly and soft." Femma's gentle touch on her head made Flora blush a deep crimson. She glanced down shyly, shuffling her feet awkwardly from side to side. As uncles of all sizes and shapes pinched her cheeks, and aunts with enveloping bosoms smothered her with hugs, she could feel her face turning permanently pink from one, and breathless from the other.

The essence of *Family* was palpable. It was as if their collective genes were floating on microscopic oxygen molecules, recognizing each other on an atomic level, breathing, and rejoicing in simply being alive.

"Oh, Mama! Look! Sophia! And she's brought Duifje!!" Flora's two cousins, their black hair similarly bobbed in the latest fashion, were walking up the street together, arm-in-arm. Dashing out the front door, Flora ran to meet them.

The trio instantly joined hands and crowded together, their voices a chorus of girlish interruptions. Each was eager to share all the gossip they thought was worth gossiping about. "My sister has a new boyfriend AND he's an opera singer!" Sophia was the first to blurt out her tantalizing tidbit of news. Christina, or Steintje as everyone called her, was ten years older than Sophia.

"He comes over to practice all the time, but I think he only shows up to make puppy eyes at Steintje." The girls giggled at the silliness of it all, but each secretly dreamed that she, too, would have boyfriends swooning over her someday. They were growing up; the signs obvious to anyone with eyes to see.

Boasting the best silver and china, the sturdy kitchen table overflowed with a veritable smorgasbord of delights: piles of *kroketten* and *bitterballen* with mustard, *poffertjes* and whipped cream, loads of cheeses, including Flora's favourite, *spikkeltjes kaas*, grainy brown breads with butter, and pickled herring. The stars of the table, three decorated cakes, each one taller and fancier than the other, were poised like Olympic athletes at the winner's podium. Ahh ... and Tante Helena's *appeltaart*! Its buttery, cinnamon aroma drew in in deep inhalations of closed eye delight from hungry admirers.

Never-before-experienced *lekkere hapjes*, decadent pieces of pressed chocolate from the van Houten Company, were passed around, a present from Oom Alexander. Oom Alex worked at van Houten's and was quite high up. The birthday twins, silver trays in hand lined with crocheted doilies, mingled amongst the crowd, graciously inviting everyone to savour a *kleine stukje* of this expensive and irresistible delicacy. Chocolate, available as powdered cocoa for baking and drinking, was the norm. Dutch cocoa, mixed with milk and sugar and served hot, was typically reserved as a special treat only for Saturdays.

The women bustled away in the kitchen, keeping all

the plates piled high while the men roamed aimlessly with mugs of beer, trying not to trip over this child or bump into that teenager. The younger men headed outside with a bottle of *jenever* in hand to escape the happy commotion.

"Let's line them all up. Come on all of you, get in order from youngest to oldest." Arranging the twins was a family tradition that took place at every event where at least two sets were in attendance.

Maurits and Max Rimini, at nine years old, were the littlest ones, so they got pushed into the line first. Their birthday was next, in December. Then Alexander and Flora, the guests of honour, were rounded up followed by Louie and Theo Mossell, also ten years old. Sixteen-year-olds Isaac and Elie Kool followed. A full head taller than their younger cousins, they were maturing into strong, young men.

Femma's twin sibling had died when not yet one year old. There was always a breadth of space in the line to honour her baby twin brother. Without a word, sisters Betty and Rachel slipped in beside Femma, Betty grasping Femma's hand with a reassuring squeeze. The Casoeto sisters: shy, identical, and inseparable.

Twenty-one-year-old Samuel Stodel, whose twin brother had been born dead, stood quietly next to Isaac, not saying much. Samuel carried an emptiness about him, a sad sort of guilt. His grey eyes rarely lifted when spoken to, and he preferred standing apart, alone, his gaze elsewhere. Like an old soul, Samuel never stopped searching for that which could make him complete, but was lost. It is intensely hard to be the survivor.

A quiet fell over the women as Louie and Theo's mother, Henriette, eyes brimming with sadness, remembered other Mossel twins, her sister's two little boys who had thrived and sprouted up like fresh grass in the spring. Then, at two-months old, one was dead, and twelve months after that, the other. The women stood, silent, each collectively mourning the carrying, birthing, nursing, loving and then losing not one child, but two. Time hesitated for a moment.

They shook off their grieving and carried on *oohing* and *ahhing* over the lengthy line of twins. Some with faces so identical it was impossible to tell the difference; others so opposite you wondered if they were related at all.

Flora found it irritating to be sandwiched in between all those boys, hers an unescapable world of them! How fabulous to have her cousins Sophia and Duifje to balance things out in her favour for a change.

The Twin Line soon disbanded, scattering siblings and cousins in all directions. The eating, conversation and laughter ramped up to the same volume as before the proud family display.

In an embarrassed dance, Flora mumbled a few words to her friends, and politely excused herself. She popped upstairs to her room, urgently needing to use the chamber pot discreetly stored under her bed.

Squatting, she glanced down. Confused, she almost tipped herself over at the sight. "NO! How horrible! This isn't supposed to happen, not to me, not yet." The stain told a different story, one of childhood, gone. Flora stood, her soiled underpants falling around her ankles. The crying began, not a sob or a wail, but a releasing of tears, a quiet mourning.

Her big sister, Greta, was fourteen, and they shared a room, so Flora understood what was what. "I'm barely now, today, ten years old," a plea uttered to the wall between more tears, "I don't know what to do and it's our birthday and there's an entire house full of people here!"

Sorrow evolved into a paralyzed panic as she realized she really didn't have a clue what to do.

A soft knock at the door, and Femma entered. "Is everything okay? I thought I heard crying. Can I ..." Eyeing the scene, her face softened in sympathy. A brief rummage through Greta's things and Femma found what she needed to tidy Flora up. "Stay here. I'll go get your mother."

As she fussed over her, Flora couldn't bring herself to say a word to the much admired older cousin, and certainly never wanted to leave her room or speak to anyone, ever, about any of this. But there was no way to stop everyone still milling downstairs from learning about it. She was going to be humiliated. And on their birthday! Why did this have to happen to her? Why now? Tears— stinging up again.

Another knock at the door and around the corner peered Duifje and Sophia. "What are you doing up here? It's almost time for presents!" Duifje walked right up, straightened her round, black-rimmed glasses, and stared Flora in the face. "Have you been crying? What's going on?"

Flora crumpled on the bed in a despondent heap, hugging her legs into a ball. "It started. Out of nowhere. You know, that thing that happens to girls and women." Perhaps Duifje didn't know, as she didn't have any sisters.

"Oh THAT," piped up Sophia. "My sister told me all about THAT. It hasn't happened to me yet, and I never want it to! It sounds perfectly awful and so not fair." She squished her face, shoulders shaking in disgust.

"Well ... I have it," announced Duifje, causing both Sophia and Flora to fling their heads in her direction, astonished. "I've had it now for over a year. It's not so bad." She seemed all at once to be the grown-up one in the group. "Pretty messy and funny smelling, but it's the best excuse for staying home from school and not having to help with housework!"

Another intrusion! This time not accompanied by a soft, timid knock, but a sudden bursting-in of informed and concerned females. In an instant, Flora was surrounded by those who loved her the deepest, cared for her the most, and would protect her as best they could, for as long as they could.

"You won't tell anyone, will you?" Her eyes darted around the room anxiously, the question a tad late considering the size and gender of the crowd buzzing in the tiny bedroom.

"No, sweetheart, we won't tell. It's a womanly secret we all share. Men stumble around such things."

Familiar faces hovered, their years of wisdom offering comments to cheer the woman-child huddled on the bed. Eyes dried. Peace restored. Panic averted.

Once back downstairs, Sophia handed Duifje her present—a hand-bound daily journal adorned with miniature purple violets on a soft cloth cover, and filled with lined, elegant, gilt-edged pages. Journals were all the rage for young girls these days; fancy diaries, with a place at the back for autographs. All the local bookshops sold them. Flora was ecstatic. Her guests signed it, each one putting in a poem, or a bit of advice, or a silly rhyme, just for her.

Her one-decade celebration had unexpectedly turned into a grown-up, unforgettable day. She couldn't help but wonder what the next ten years of her life would bring.

1984 - CALGARY

GO FIGURE

*I*nstinct hinted that I was pregnant with my second child even before testing positive at the doctor's office. My middle swelled and my clothes shrank a mere ten days past the date of my last period.

The nurse—older, crotchety, disgruntled—observed me with a disapproving frown, "Do you *want* this baby?"

Jonathan, my firstborn, was ten months old. "Of course." My retaliatory defensive response goaded on by her piercing eyes and the uncalled-for redundancy of the question.

This was a planned pregnancy; unlike the surprise of my first one, which abruptly stymied my studies at the University of Calgary in musicology and piano performance.

With my first pregnancy, I suffered terrible nausea, throwing up five, six times a day, every day, every week, every month. Sometimes I was lucky enough to get my head in the toilet on time but at other times, not quite, vomiting all over the bathtub or floor, or out the door of the car after desperately requesting an emergency road stop. I was still throwing up on the delivery table.

My mother didn't experience any morning sickness whatsoever, nor did she suffer any stretch marks. With no family females to commiserate with, I often wondered what my grandmothers' pregnancies had been like. My two great-grandmothers between them birthed twenty-four children — couldn't have been too terrible.

This pregnancy was no different. It arrived with the same relentless level of nausea as the first. Something as simple as a walk outside gave no respite. I threw up on the sidewalk, barely missing little Jonathan in his blue-striped umbrella stroller, purchased on sale for $9.95 at the Zellers in Calgary.

Oh, God! I hope it's twins. I can't go through this again! My poor stomach grew bigger by the day, by the minute, or so a vain attempt to see past my bulge would indicate, my size-ten feet disappearing beneath me.

A favourite maternity dress, one I sewed for myself out of black polyester fabric ornamented with large, lime green polka-dots, transformed me into a replica of the spotty, big-footed waddling beast from Dr. Seuss's book, *Put Me in the Zoo.* I think I still have that dress somewhere. Maybe I should turn it into a bedspread.

BP — Before Pregnancy — I flaunted a perfect, enviable figure. That 36-24-36 that turned men's heads and made other women glare at me. By my eighth month, I measured 38-82-40. The only head turning was mine, straight towards the toilet. Stating that I was enormous was an understatement!

Friends who hadn't seen me in a while would involuntarily blurt out, "Good heavens, what happened to you?" But no, the ultrasound showed only one baby, one heartbeat. I secretly hoped it was wrong. Such equipment was not nearly so sophisticated and accurate as now. The image on the screen resembled something more amoeba and blob-like than human. I couldn't make out anything, let alone two of something.

March 25, 1984, 4:00 p.m. A comforting cup of steaming hot Earl Grey tea in hand, I reach forward for a piece of remaining Christmas fruitcake from the pile artistically displayed on my favourite blue and white flowered china plate when *POP*—my water broke, soaking the couch. Although not due for another three-and-a-half weeks, Michael Timothy, healthy and single, greeted the world at 5:01 a.m. on the morning of March 26.

Odd what you remember. My then husband, true to nature, became embroiled in an argument with the head nurse. To escape the both of them, I snuck out to the hospital bathroom. Michael was almost born on the toilet!

No twins for me. Just stretch marks from neck to knees.

GHOSTS

"*W*here are we off to today?" Looking forward to yet another memorable day in Holland, my mother and I started out the door of Tante Zulma's house, then strolled north along the picturesque tree-lined canal.

I imagined the same scene in Spring; bursts of bright rainbow tulips nodding egg-shaped heads from manicured, miniature front gardens. My mother had planted drifts of tulips in our flowerbeds back in Saskatchewan. The yellow ones seemed toughest, able to survive long, frigid prairie winters, just waiting for the return of the sun. As a little girl, bent over double, face to the ground, I would scour the frozen earth for days, hunting for their return. Miraculously, there would be that one perfect day when shy little red tulip noses would just start poking out. Life, reincarnated again.

We headed to the intercity train stop, which would take us into the heart of Amsterdam. Not getting an immediate answer, I asked once more where we were going.

"To see some relatives," Mom replied. Here we go again. More mysterious relatives, more people to match up with faces, places and genetics. I didn't have a clue about any of them. Yet, somehow, all these pre-existing relatives knew everything about me. That wasn't fair.

"Who are they?" Distracted, I tossed a few green, narrow willow leaves into the canal as we walked along, my voice betraying a slight hint of annoyance and boredom. I wondered how many more odd relatives there could possibly be.

"Some of mine," the strained nonchalance of my mother's response carried a tone intimating no further questions.

But wait ... all my mother's relatives lived in Australia. Who were these, where did they come from, and why was I never told anything about them? What am I supposed to say when I meet them? "Oh, hello. I'm Stella. I'm so sorry, but I've never heard of you. And what relationship are you to me again?" I kept my thoughts to myself.

My mother waltzed her way on foot around Old Amsterdam with ease, despite her absence of over three decades. The streets of a city, built over 1,000 years ago via a series of canals, do not change. So long as one's memory is sound, the body finds its own way home.

A slightly balding, shortish gentleman greeted us at the door with surprising exuberance. "Come in, *Fietje*, come in!" We both found ourselves enveloped by massive hugs and noisy kisses, one for each cheek. Beaming, he turned to me, "I'm Jacob, your mother's cousin, and this is my wife, Rebecca. Come, I'm taking all of us out for lunch."

Jacob
Rebecca

Their names resonated and bounced around my wondering brain before settling into that place of subconscious awareness where the nebulous resolves into the obvious. These were Jewish relatives. Dutch Jewish relatives. Living in Amsterdam in their late sixties in 1978.

Lunch? A blur.

MY MOTHER DELIGHTED in participating in what social opportunities existed in our small Saskatchewan rural town, miles away from any other town. She loved meeting new people and making new friends. Her circle encompassed any and every one from all walks of life, every background and culture.

A veritable United Nations, representing countries from around the world, concentrated itself on seven square miles of hot prairie grass in the middle of nowhere: Ukrainian, Chinese, Korean, Japanese, Jamaican, Norwegian, Swedish, Dutch, British, Irish, Scottish, American, East Indian, Egyptian, Swedish, German, French, and Jewish. Everyone living and raising families together; celebrating their chosen new world while still honouring the old.

Accompanying this vast multi-cultural landscape was food. Lots of food. Every kind of food! Any visit to any of my mother's many friends, in accordance with the laws of old-fashioned small town hospitality, had to be accompanied by food: mountains of Swedish meatballs, smelly lutefisk on hard, rye bread, fragrant curry, smoked turkey sandwiches, crepes and pancakes, homemade pickles, jams and jellies, cherry blintzes, oily latkes, eye-tempting cakes, cookies and pies.

We had exotic food at our household as well, things that none of my friends seemed to have. Some clearly Dutch pantry items, as I could read the Dutch labels, but also two items in particular, with labels written in completely unrecognizable non-English characters. One was a box of unusually large, flat crackers that had an odd looking candlestick with seven candles on the front and another, a box of soup mix with a picture of round, yellow dumpling-like balls floating in the soup.

"What's for supper"? I would ask.

"Soep met balletjes," my mother would reply, always with a grin and always commenting that that is what her mother would say when asked the same question. Where on earth such odd food items could be acquired in Estevan, Saskatchewan was a mystery.

But they must have been for sale somewhere in town, as, to my great surprise, I saw the exact same flat crackers once when I went to a church service with a friend. There they were—my mother's favourite snack— broken into small pieces and passed around for the contrite to "partake of" during the service. I liked my mother's version better—big, crispy chunks smeared with butter, and sprinkled liberally with brown sugar.

A vivid, very early childhood memory also involved food, and me not wanting to go with my mother as she benevolently delivered a pot of homemade soup to a creepy old man living alone in a dark, filthy house. We had gone there before, which is why I knew I did not want to go again. But off we went, me, two-and-a-half years old, dressed in a white blouse and pleated woollen plaid skirt of blue, grey, and red, and sporting a fresh, done-by-Mom, bobbed haircut, bangs slightly aslant. My mother was sincere and genuine in her desire to care for the less fortunate and the elderly, a gift she inherited from her mother.

Especially kind-hearted friends of ours were Leon and Dora Dragushan and Dora's spinster sister, Ruth. Although not yet educated in the world's many philosophical variations at the age of eight, I knew the Dragushans were Jewish, whatever that meant. Their furniture was covered in plastic (super icky to sit on in the summer), and they owned a women's clothing store downtown. Perhaps those were key identifiers.

Childless themselves, it gave them tremendous pleasure to fuss over us. Mrs. Dragushan suffered from polio when very young and walked with an obvious limp. Hearing other children at school laugh and make fun of her made my heart sad, as she was such an extraordinary person in my life.

One evening my parents invited them over for dinner. A classic Dutch dish is *snert*, or pea soup, which we ate for supper at least once a week growing up, and possibly the best item in my mother's cooking repertoire. Although rather vile-looking stuff with its mealy, thick texture, green colour, and meat bits floating about, it was tasty and filling. The Dutch prefer practical, simple fare.

Everyone sits down for dinner—my family of five and our three Dragushan guests. I had been tasked with setting the dinner table. On display—our best china and silverware, ironed linen napkins, and sterling candlesticks. Everything was perfectly elegant and lovely.

Out comes my mother from the kitchen with brimming hot bowls of Dutch *snert*. Silver spoons dip up, then down. Exclamations of "how delicious" and "how savoury" accompany smacking mouthfuls. Little me, wishing to contribute to the conversation and educate our guests on the chosen menu, exclaims loudly, "You'll never guess what's in the soup ... PIG'S FEET!!"

I feel an instantaneous, swift, and not subtle kick, and my mother is shooting daggers at me across the table with her eyes. Thoroughly confused, I go quiet and say nothing more; any memory of the remainder of the evening erased by the pain in my ankle.

Decades later, upon reflection, I came to understand the "why" of that abrupt knee-jerk reaction, and realized what my mother had done, and realized that she knew what she had done, too. I was not the one deserving of such a kick. That bowl of soup housed a story, a truth, and a lie all ladled into one.

WE SPENT a memorable day with Jacob and Rebecca Hijman laughing at jokes, enduring good-natured teasing and eating plenty of food. This newly discovered first cousin of my mother was funny, exuberant, generous, loving, and brimming with life. He interacted with her as if she had never left Holland, as if she was still family living right down the street, and had been for all these past years.

The day over, while walking home, I spoke up in a style and tone entirely out of character for me. "Oom Jacob and Tante Becca are Jewish," I stated rather than questioned, "no one other than Jewish people are named Jacob and Rebecca."

And, in a style completely out of character for her, almost resignedly my mother replied, "Yes, they are." There was no further clarification of her answer, no offering up of a tidbit of a childhood memory as might be expected when revealing so vast a thing as religiously specific relatives for the first time.

"So, if Oom Jacob is your first cousin, and he has the same last name as your mother's maiden name, then he is the son of your mother's brother," my new skill of dissecting family relationships now sharply honed, I added, "so your mother must have been Jewish, too."

In a split second, she came back at me, her voice strident with an unexpected, insistent, and lashing response, "NO! My mother was NOT Jewish. According to the Germans, she was Italian because she married an Italian."

My parents had not been born in Canada and rarely spoke English to each other. Growing up, naturally I was curious and fascinated about where they came from. How exotic having parents from Holland, the land of tulips and windmills, and exquisite blue and white tiles. I even spoke a little Dutch such as, *Wil je een kopje thee* and *Ben je helemaal gek?* (swear words not the only tidbits in my non-English repertoire).

Hmm, okay. I don't think your ethnicity changes at the altar. I did know that my maternal grandfather was of Italian background, so no surprise there.

Giovanni Antonio Vittali. You can't get much more Italian than that. His children, including my mother, all had Italian names: Christina Elisabeth, Antonio Pietro, Sophia Maria, and the baby, another Giovanni Antonio. I grew up believing, not because I was told mind you, but more of an assumption, that my maternal grandmother was, simply, Dutch.

In keeping with my strict upbringing, I did not argue or disagree with my mother's analysis of her mother's background. I said nothing further, not relishing a kick in the ankle at the age of eighteen any more than I did at the age of eight. We walked along in silence.

But after a few minutes, my mother surprised me. She offered up information, matching what was already simmering in the back of my mind. Her mother, she divulged, came from an extensive family, and perhaps, to protect me from a more horrifically larger truth, she merely said, "They all died in the war, except for a few."

Oom Jacob had to be brimming with life, out of obligation and necessity. He was shouldering the burden of needing to carry on living for entire generations of people that were not.

LIES

*W*hat a glorious, out-of-character July day. White drifts of clouds lazing across a sapphire sky lifted Sophia's spirit by their freshness, their purity. Blue and white — the very essence of Holland.

She was dreaming out her window again; the soot-smeared panes of poured glass blurring the twisted cruelty of lives enacted below. Only in her imagination was life still beautiful, as it had been when she was little, the sweet memories of an innocent past blurring, its colours bleeding like a street painting abandoned in the rain.

A familiar voice calling up the stairs broke the mood, forcing her mind back to reality and into the mundane.

"Run into town for me, *schatje boetje*, and buy today's ration of bread and milk."

"Yes, Mama. I'll be down in a minute."

Always the errand girl. Her younger brother, Joe, too small at age seven to be of any use, and twenty-year-old Tony surly and dismissive with little time for a pestering younger sister. Tony worked long hours in the family business, although many evenings, even when the work was done, Sophia wondered why he did not come home.

She adored her older sister Christina, twenty-four, but her clandestine adult life was far from Sophia's sixteen-year-old view. Christina had changed. Her fiancée, a locally famous opera singer, was gone; taken and deported without warning. The young couple were robbed of any goodbyes. Ever since, her mood was irritable and her words short. Day after day she would come home from work at the Nestelroy paper factory down the street, lock herself in her bedroom, and do nothing but write in her journal. When she did appear, too often Sophia could tell that her sister had been crying.

"Smile and appear confident when you go out." Betje Vittali lived in a permanent state of unease, every day a tightrope of mere existence. She fussed nervously with Sophia's collar. "Be friendly, but don't speak and don't stop." Taking the ration coupons handed to her, Sophia folded them in quarters, and shoved them deep inside her skirt pocket.

"Do you have your whistle with you, the one Tony gave you?" An exasperated nod. "Good girl. Now be back as quickly as you can, stay on the main streets, and away from the canals." Her eyes rolled at the all too familiar juvenile instructions. "One more thing," Sophia's mother shot her youngest daughter a stern, foreboding look. "If a soldier stops to question you and asks how old you are, what do you say?"

Lying used to bother the pretty, petite girl with the delicate, white skin and tiny freckles. She was forced to lie—about her age, about so many things. She wished the opposite, to say she was older than she was. After four war years of practice, she was now an expert at disguising and hiding the truth, and had become skillfully adept at guarding secrets under the ironic guise of youth and innocence.

"I'm twelve." Sophia dutifully mumbled out her expected reply.

Truth had lost its purpose years ago, the covering of it as necessary for life as heavy clothes against a December frost. Naïveté had also long since disappeared. The stark risk to older girls posed by lonely soldiers far from home and family well understood, and too often suffered.

A kiss on the cheek and down the stairs she went, her mother's gaze memorizing the moment: the curly bounce of her precious daughter's glossy black hair, the swish of her flower-print cotton summer skirt, until Sophia opened the door and disappeared out into the street.

Pangs of guilt accompanied Betje. Standing on the landing alone and inert, her eyes filled with sadness. She hated sending Sophia out in public, into a dangerous and uncertain city. And yet she did. Sophia's leaving and her staying was emotionally paralyzing; she was powerless.

Condemned to wear the yellow Star of David, Mrs. Vittali bent under its oppressive weight each time she left the comfort and safety of her home. She was somewhat protected from German intrusion, but only by virtue of her Dutch-Italian husband; easier to remain cloistered inside, quarantined by choice, than to risk everyone and everything.

An even darker, more gnawing form of guilt plagued these long, tense days. Hers was a nebulous safety, whereas most of her brothers and sisters, along with their families, had been dragged off to an unknown fate. Levie Hijman, the patriarch, her father, willingly volunteering himself as a concentration camp worker, despite his age. He was desperate to be with his sons, three out of the four having already been deported. His sudden leaving caused pangs of abandonment and hopelessness in his grown children left behind.

Mina, her sister-in-law, married to Giovanni's brother, Paulus, also taken. She had been betrayed, sought out, and arrested. Arrested for what? Being a Jewess? Being a woman? Being childless? Betrayal requires no reasonable cause, no justification for its devices. And betrayed by a Dutchman no less, one notorious for hunting out Jews and handing them over to the enemy for a price.

How will everyday life ever be possible again? How can one live with such people when the war is over? For it will be over, one day, someday. There will come that day when the sun rises on an occupied country and sets on a freed one. Betje pushed such disconcerting thoughts behind her with the closing of the door.

Sophia was elated to be outside, free, and on her own, the thrill of it eclipsing danger. The sunshine lazing from above warmed her spirit and was far more glorious than the diffused beams previously filtering through a dusty bedroom window.

Amsterdam was her city, and she loved it. Ancient canals with towering lindens paid homage at the water's flat banks while willows dipped graceful, leafy fingertips into gently moving currents. Side streets sheltered tiny flower stalls and tall-paned bakery shops, enticing fragrances from both wafting through the narrow pathways. Sophia breathed deeply, the familiar scents and scenes long imprinted into the pulse and rhythm of her daily life.

People smiled in passing, each person welcoming the reassurance of familiar faces. German and Dutch soldiers blankly patrolled the ancient cobblestone streets, their postures devoid of purpose; non-aligned artificial allies thrown together by political force. There were no smiles in their direction, only blind avoidance.

Sophia, too, ignored them, a determined mood of forced confidence in her steps. One soldier let out a low whistle as she passed, his cigarette falling to the ground at the exhalation of toned air. "Hey there, you're a sweet thing." A German. How despicable. *"Willst du eine Tasse Kaffee mit mir?"* Face forward, head tossed back, she quickened her walk, tense fingers gripping the whistle in her pocket, the callous laughter of the soldiers drowning out the pounding in her chest.

"Goedemorgen Miss Vittali, you're looking extra lovely today. Are you here for your usual order?" Blushing, Sophia smiled up at the kindly face of her uncle, white-aproned behind his familiar bakery counter. She nodded, handing over the tightly folded blue ration ticket retrieved from her pocket.

"Isn't that sun just marvellous? We don't get sun like that too often. And how is your mother? It's been days, no, weeks, since she's been here." Ordinary small-talk filled the air between them.

Sophia paused for the briefest of moments as an image of her mother with that cursed star on her chest flashed through her mind. She was ashamed of that image. And she burned with shame at herself for not wanting her mother with her whenever she went out. She vowed never to be branded as others in her family had been, ever, in her life, not ever.

"My mother's well, thank you." A perfunctory reply, uttered while holding out her empty cloth bag and hating the impression of beggary that accompanied it. "Mama says to make sure we receive our full share. There are six of us. Plus Papa is always dragging some poor person or other home for dinner, and my brothers are constantly whining and complaining."

Sophia's eyes wandered around the small shop, its bleak shelves and empty racks themselves hungry-looking. Her growling stomach remembered trips to the bakery before the war when, with a wink and a grin, her uncle would sneak a savoury, still warm *saucijzenbroodje* into her bag. Her mouth began watering at the merest thought of a bite of sausage.

"The allowed amount of bread per person is even lower than before, my child. I cannot do more." He braved a smile. "But for you, I give my freshest and best." Handing his attractive Italian-looking niece her bag, now filled with the family's war-allotted bread ration, he waved her on, eyes riveted until she was out of view. "Lucky girl," he reflected aloud, a faintly sour note of bitterness in his words, "I wonder if she has any idea how lucky."

Thankfully, the soldiers previously haunting the streets had wandered elsewhere to practice their intimidation. Letting down her guard, Sophia relaxed her pace and sauntered alongside the canal, stopping to gaze into its stillness.

Mated pairs of ducks nibbled at luxuriant green water grasses, their bodies hovering motionless on the surface, while an invisible antithesis of webbed feet paddled incessantly below.

Tearing the smallest bit off the bottom of one of her loaves, she tossed it towards the nonchalant birds. A breeze floated the crumb's weightlessness ever so slightly before depositing the morsel atop the blue of the canal. In a flash, with a violent spontaneous neck extension, one mallard gobbled it up. "So it is with all of us," she mused, "swallowed in an instant by unseen forces bigger than ourselves."

Sophia considered sneaking in a clandestine visit to see her favourite aunt, Tante Mina. Mina treated her with such kindness and love, as if Sophia was her daughter, not a niece. Could she secretly make it there and back and still be home in time?

The bright sunny day was pulling people out into the streets in great numbers, putting the already guarded SS soldiers in a foul mood, their chiseled faces scowling in disapproval. Sophia swept the idea of a sneak visit to her aunt's house from her mind. It was too great a risk for both of them.

She was, though, right around the corner from her cousin Duifje's house. She dared venture past, peering into the lower floor living room window. All was dark. Sheets, dusty and ghost-like, covered the furniture. Sophia's father had been left in charge of the house and kept his eye on it to make sure no one broke in and stole anything. Sophia missed Duifje so much. It had been ten months since she and her family had gone to work in the labour camps. *How was she managing?* Sophia wondered. *And what about Flora, her twin cousin? How come neither of them ever wrote any letters?*

Heading into a familiar side street, she hunted for Meneer van der Tuuk and his milk wagon, drawn by his old, black Frisian horse, Cinder. They should be nearing her house by now. Hearing the rhythmic *clop clop clop* of horse's hooves, she turned towards the sound and rounded the corner.

Voices. Male voices! Urgent yet muffled, insistent but hushed. Sophia nervously stepped back against an old, brick building to listen in the shadows, her heart pounding again. She knew these voices. They belonged to her father and brother.

"We have won the bid for three new renovation contracts with the city. This is the opportunity we have been waiting for. Now it will be easy to hide anything."

"Yes, but if we are caught? Can we rely on the workers?"

"No, they must never know. Not that we cannot trust them, they are all are loyal, hard-working and honest. But at gunpoint, a man tells all, and even more, to save himself and his family."

Giovanni's voice darkened as he met the brooding eyes of his eldest son. "This we do ourselves. The responsibility has been entrusted to us and is on our backs. You. And me."

Shortly after the Nazi's military takeover of Amsterdam, Sophia recalled multiple strange visits from now-deported relatives, neighbours, and sometimes, complete strangers. Clandestine arrivals, occurring without invitation, pulled hastily into her father's study.

They left as silently as they came. No tea, no pleasantries, no stopping to tousle the curls of little Joe. Only clouded faces, torn voices, and wild eyes; hands, previously thrust possessively in coats and bags, now visible and empty.

Secrets laced with lies. Everywhere. Everyone. How does telling a lie morph from a social evil into a required good?

Rations procured, Sophia arrived home to find her mother and father sitting at the kitchen table. 11:00 a.m. coffee. Comfort in the worst of times—the smallest of pleasures creating some semblance of routine.

She passed her mother the bread and milk

accompanied by a kiss on the cheek before abruptly turning to escape up the stairs.

"Sophia."

Her father's deep voice rang in her ears for the second time that morning.

"Yes, Papa?" Glancing casually at a miniature painting of a young girl sporting a red wool hat, she averted her eyes, afraid to reveal the new truths guiltily hiding in them.

"You are to go on your bicycle to Uithoorn. I have a coil of construction rope that should be a fair trade for meat or vegetables with any farmer on the road."

"But Papa!" Whirling around, eyes flashing in protest, Sophia's adolescent fears vanished in light of this new parental demand. "My bicycle has no tires, only rims. And Uithoorn is an hour's ride away. It will be horrible and bumpy and … "

"Houd je grote bek dicht!" He turned on her in a sudden flare of temper. "Our family is half-starving, your mother ekes out our rations to the last crumb, and you dare complain about a bumpy bicycle when all I ask is for you to do a simple task on behalf of the family? Do you have any idea what everyone else does around here while you whine upstairs in your room, primping in front of the mirror and pining away like some sorry lovesick cow? Who do you think you are, the Princess of Amsterdam?" Words piled on words, piling on pain.

Sophia dared not look up, the sharp sword of his voice cutting into her heart. *Why is he always so angry at me? This goddamn war is not my fault.* A sideways hopeful glance at her mother revealed Giovanni's wife busying herself with housework, as if her daughter was not suffering under an Italian rage. Theirs was a home under patriarchal rule.

Eyes brimming, she pulled herself to face him. "Yes, Papa, I'll go. If I leave now, I can be back by dark."—a conciliatory response uttered with controlled acquiescence.

Sophia bolted up to her room and slammed the door. *I hate him. When I am older, and this is all over, I'm getting as far away from here as I can.*

The road to Uithoorn was narrow, gravelled, and rutted. With all available rubber supplies redirected to the war effort, bicycle tires were rare, a luxury from the past that one only dared dream about now in the present. Riding on rims was tortuous.

The massive coil of earthy-smelling, oil-stained construction rope draped across her left shoulder hung precariously over her back. Rough, scratchy fibres bit mercilessly into her skin with every pedal shift, chafing through her thin jacket. Sophia feared if she fell off, she would never get up again.

Forty minutes after leaving Amsterdam, she spotted a farm on the right. How different from a city house. The thatched roof, grey with weather and age, shielded small windows recessed deep into the thick walls, its drooping overhangs guarding the interior from sun and wind.

A small flock of eight Drenthe Heath sheep grazed nearby, their gaze pausing mid-munch only briefly as she rode past. A sturdy tree in the front yard served well as a bicycle stand, allowing her to dismount with some level of safety. Still clothed in rope, she approached.

Her knuckles rapped boldly on the ancient timber door, itself an oak relic from past lumbered forests long transformed into sailing ships, their destiny realized at the bottom of the North Sea.

"Goede middag mevrouw. Wat kan ik voor jou doen?" A

plumpish woman in her mid-forties cautiously cracked open the door, suspiciously eyeing this uninvited visitor.

Sophia started in, her voice a timid but convincing tone, "I have a strong coil of rope here, perfect for heavy farm use. Would you have some food to trade? Our family in Amsterdam is practically starving."

"My husband is not here. We have no need for rope. I'm sorry." Her face, betraying the barest semblance of pity, faded as the door closed with a formidable creak. Sophia stood and stared at its frame, the burden on her shoulders abruptly heavier. The sheep stared as she hoisted herself back on her bicycle and continued down the dirt road.

Two more farms met her. Two more times, she struggled down from her crippled transportation. One house was completely dark. The other sent her running for her life as its owner yelled from the barn, brandishing a rusty hoe, "Go back to the city, you selfish beggar. I'm sick of being harassed with pillows, candlesticks, silver, and trinkets. I have nothing for you and have my own family to feed."

Driven by hunger and fear of her father's rage, Sophia rallied to carry on. One more farm. Surely someone will be kind. One more awkward descent. One more knock on an unwelcoming door.

"You won't find anyone in these parts with any food to trade for goods, my dear." At least the voice was benevolent, if nothing else. Sophia stared at the ground, tears welling up in her eyes. It had been a day of tears. "So many people come here from Amsterdam," the voice continued, "all the farms have given what they can. Nothing is left. Go home."

Despondent and still trapped in the coiled rope like a python's prey, Sophia climbed up on her bicycle one last time, turned and pedalled north, away from the quiet of the farmlands. The lowering sun coloured the countryside in shades of burnished gold. Wisps of cloud blushed pink at the edges as day neared its end. She would have to hurry to reach home before dark.

With every push, her legs ached. Blisters caused by constant friction against the hard bicycle seat began oozing and bleeding through her underwear. She craved the tiny piece of bread thrown to the ducks earlier in the day, that bright sunny, lazy part of the day, when life was free and unburdened.

Anger eclipsed pain as she grumbled at this impossible task pushed upon her. Papa would not understand and would rage at her failures—again.

Unexpectedly, a tall man appeared on the road, his shadow giant in the evening light. Arms waving wildly over his head, he ran straight at her, shouting and yelling, forcing Sophia to the side of the road.

Oh my God oh my God oh my God! reverberated in her head as she frantically tried to keep her balance. The bicycle swerved uncontrollably, lop-siding the heavy rope and crashing her to the ground. Terror-struck, she lay bruised and scraped in the gravel, unable to move. She spotted her whistle, somehow thrown from her pocket, out of reach.

He loomed over her, a black spectre blocking the light. Sophia, powerless, felt his weathered hands on her shoulders, and the stench of sheep dung on his clothes.

"Oh my, are you all right?" The farmer detangled her from the bicycle and helped her to her feet. "I'm so sorry. I just needed to get your attention. Are you the girl who stopped by earlier today with some rope?"

Sophia's mind whirled in confusion at the shock of falling off her bicycle, this sudden terrifying encounter, and now being asked about that damned, burdensome, unwanted rope. Bits of crushed stone, embedded in her thighs and knees, stung like bees, and her right arm was bleeding through her ripped jacket sleeve.

"I think I'm okay." Trembling, Sophia brushed dirt off her skirt, its delicate flower print now streaked with mud and the once meticulously ironed fabric sadly wrinkled. The rope, uncoiled, lay in a heap on the ground. Straightening up, she recognized the first farmhouse with its oak door and lazily grazing sheep.

"My wife told me a girl came by looking to trade rope for food. I need rope. Haven't been able to find any in weeks." Sophia stared, speechless, still shaking from her fall. "Well, let's get you to the house, get you all sorted, and help you on your way."

They walked across the road to the farmhouse where the farmer's wife, now all smiles and helping hands, took Sophia in and washed her up. A bowl of soup, some bread and cheese, and she was ready to go, elated at her success and the relinquishing of her burden.

The sheep farmer held out a filthy burlap sack joined at the top with a knot of twine, its long loose ends dangling down the sides. *What was this?* She wondered. Whatever it was, it was alive! Something inside was writhing furiously.

"What's in the bag?" she asked, wide-eyed.

The man grinned a toothless smile back at her. "A rooster! He's a bit scrawny, but we can spare 'im."

"Aren't you doing to ... umm ... kill it first?"

"Helemaal niet! It would be all maggots by the time you got it home if I did. Don't worry. I've tied his legs together. He can't escape." The farmer began tying the sack around her waist while the bird inside convulsed furiously.

What? She never imagined this. She assumed a trade for potatoes, a few cabbages, or perhaps a tasty mix of carrots and parsnips. A sack of ground whole wheat flour would be luxurious but a live rooster?

Sophia desperately wished she could escape. At least that horrible rope, however uncomfortable, had stayed put. Now she had a very much alive, wing-flapping, crowing, insane chicken tied to her.

The rest of the trip was sheer hell. As she entered Amsterdam, onlookers laughed and pointed. What a sight! Her pain, fury, and agony was coupled with humiliation.

Back home at last, she parked her bicycle under the lamppost in front of their canal house on the Amsteldijk. Sophia and the now quiet, hapless bird, its energy spent from fruitless thrashings inside the sagging captive sack, headed up the stairs.

Betje Vittali untied the twisted binder twine holding the bag around her daughter's waist, grabbed the tied feet of Mr. Rooster, and walked him, upside down, into the kitchen, wings dangling unceremoniously. A honed kitchen knife glinted in the fading daylight as Betje, with one swift movement, chopped off the rooster's head. There he lay, decapitated, bleeding out in the sink.

Sophia gaped in horror. How could one so gentle and kind, so full of love and generosity, ruthlessly and without hesitation, take a life, even if that life belonged to a lowly chicken? How could it be so easy to be a normal person one minute carrying on everyday life and the next, a bloodthirsty murderer?

It was ridiculous, she realized, as of course animals had to be killed, but it seemed, these days, no one was normal anymore. People turned into beasts at the tiniest provocation. Observing this in her mother was too much for her.

Alone in her room at last, Sophia buried her face in her pillow and cried relentlessly; long sobs, their hard wails muffled by the soft cotton of the pillowcase. She missed school and friends, parties and new clothes, apple tarts and butter. She missed her adoring aunts, her cousins, and her dear Opa, all of them long gone, lost somewhere in this miserable war. Her cries poured out a deep mourning for what her life should have been.

"Fietje, Johannetje. Time for supper!" Their mother's voice—normal, routine. Little Joe ran down the hall and pounded on his sister's bedroom door. Sophia pulled herself up to let him in.

"Fie, Fie, Fie! Chicken for dinner! Chicken for dinner! Come come come come!!" Two pudgy, grubby little hands grabbed hers, his innocent eyes shining wide with hungry anticipation. Sophia indulged his enthusiasm, feigning equal eagerness as little Joe dragged her down the stairs, and back into the merciless reality of their war-occupied world.

MINA

"*T*oday we are going to visit the person I love most in the entire world, next to my mother," declared by mother. By this length of time into our Holland vacation, the shock effect of the constant stream of Dutch relatives introduced to me had started to subside. Our new morning journey away from Tante Zulma's house on the canal involved a lengthy trek to a section of Amsterdam we had not ventured into before.

Architectural history speaks from the quaint and unique houses of Old Amsterdam. Three or four stories high, each brick building sports its own unusual rooftop gable design, with descriptive names such as Neck, Spout, or Step identifying specific styles and significance, not only of the history of the building, but also its age.

I had never seen anything like these houses, joined yet distinctly separate, and stretching for entire blocks. The fairy-tale rooftops sported arms extending from the topmost exterior out-facing wall, each bearing an impressive iron hook destined to haul up heavy furniture otherwise impossible to manoeuvre through the steep, confined interior staircases. The houses were houses inside of houses; most levels a self-contained home with a separate stairwell skirting everyone's privacy yet connecting them all.

Estevan, a young pup of a town inaugurated as a city in 1957, boasted bungalows as the house plan of choice; plain, predictable and more straightforward for moving into and out of. And definitely no houses in rows, connected like Lego blocks, with families living one on top of the other.

Great-aunt Mina Vittali lived on the ground floor of a gabled canal house, narrow, but extending a long way back, with each living space disappearing one after the other in a long line to the end. Natural light absent, the rooms, made ponderous by dark wood furnishings, cast a gloomy shadow save for the front sitting area with its bowed-out picture window. Her house, sandwiched between two adjoining houses, naturally had no windows on any of the side walls.

Mina was the wife of my grandfather's brother, Paulus Vittali. They were childless. What an embarrassing noise she made over me, commenting over and over again on the supposed astonishing family resemblance. "Those eyes. She has the eyes."

GRADE 5. First crush. Ricky. But he was crushing on Susan and her sun-catching waist-length auburn-red hair, not me. I did manage to get myself over to his house one day after school to watch an episode of *The Partridge Family*.

"Well, hello there. Who is this?" Ricky's mother gave me a little hug and welcomed me in. "You're the ter Hart girl, aren't you?" Everyone knows everything in a small town. "What pretty eyes you have!"

"Wow!" I thought. "Really?" I'd never given any thought to my eyes. Up to that point I'd never considered looking *at* them, only looking *out* of them. "They're so unusual," her own eyes large as she carried on staring at me, "sea green with tiny flecks of brown. And those lashes! You'll be a real beauty someday!"

Despite Ricky's mother's preference, Bambi eyes didn't win over Rapunzel hair.

MINA, my mother, and I arranged ourselves in the narrow front room overlooking the busy street and placid canal beyond. Tempting me on an oak tea caddy near the only available window sat a polished, ornate silver tray bearing fantastically delicious looking pastries smothered in whipped cream! Proper manners mandated extreme patience and self-control. The expected, appropriate behaviour, was, of course, to sit politely until offered one, all the while wondering if devouring three would be considered rude. I have an almost addictive weakness for anything with whipped cream.

On the corner of 4th Street and Souris Avenue in downtown Estevan stood the Tasty Bakery, right beside the Orpheum Movie Theatre. The most eye-catching and mouth-watering delicacies tortured me from the bakery window: gooey, flakey butter tarts, delicately iced sugar cookies, triple-decker slices of vanilla cake smothered in marshmallow frosting, whole apple pies. And eclairs. Oh, the eclairs!

Fresh, cream-filled eclairs dusted with powdered sugar were $0.25 in 1970, an unattainable fortune for a ten-year-old. No such thing as a family allowance in those days, and any cooking, washing or helping was not completed in anticipation of pennies.

Once, I snuck inside and stood by the display case for a long time, trying my best to put on a hungry and forlorn face, hoping to elicit pity and inspire a kind soul to buy me something. No such luck. When old enough to babysit and earn my own money, I proudly handed $0.25 over in exchange for a mouthful of heaven anytime I wanted.

What a disappointment to bite into my *slagroom tartje*, after waiting and sitting in the near dark at Tante Mina's house for what felt like an interminable length of time, only for my eager taste buds to discover no sugar or vanilla in the cream. Score "1" for the Tasty Bakery!

Quite a bit of tea was necessary to wash down the lack-lustre pastry, and soon the next room to explore was the bathroom which was, literally, a water closet—a minuscule space. Quietly, I snuck away.

Horrified, I could not figure out how to flush the archaic contraption of a toilet. A long rope dangling from the ceiling gave the impression of being useful, but no matter which way I yanked, pulled, or twisted the darn thing, it stubbornly refused to flush anything down. Sheepish, I had no choice but to emerge from captivity and beg for help. Tante Mina laughed, not at me, but because of me. A single skilled jerk on the rope and ... sploosh ... away everything went, thank goodness!

A timeless, unbreakable bond existed between aunt and niece; theirs a noticeable admiration, mutual love, and sheer delight at being together again. The years fell away.

As it was obvious I could not contribute anything of substance to their intimate Dutch conversation, restless, I escaped out the back kitchen door and into the garden.

Fragrant July flowers were in glorious full bloom. Exotic lilies of every imaginable colour hovered above dainty zinnias, while exquisite roses only ever seen in florist bouquets in Estevan graced the waist-high rock wall at the edge of the house.

Glancing over, the neighbouring yard, in stark contrast, was barren and bleak with nothing but weeds and untamed hedgery. This struck me as very strange in a country renowned for its ability to break forth into bloom. Since only a few shrubs and flower beds separated the two spaces, curious, I wandered over to new territory.

Peering through tattered lace curtains hanging askew over windows knitted in cobwebs, I could make out a kitchen which, in complete contrast to my great-aunt's rich and lavishly decorated home, was a shattered disaster. Overturned chairs. A table—its legs broken, kneeling in penitence—covering shards of glass. Broken dishes. Random kitchen items scattered across the floor. A ghostly layer of dust shrouded the entire scene—startling and unsettling.

The obvious thought would be to ask what happened. But I did not, the answer already evident; another uncovered, unspoken truth. We were in the Jewish quarter. Tante Mina was Jewish. The family next door had been taken and deported, their home looted and ransacked. Who would return to pick up the abandoned pieces? No one. Not after one year, or thirty-three. There it remained; an unintended shrine to sorrow.

TANTE MINA CAME to stay with us in Saskatchewan in 1980, two summers after our trip to Holland. I remember vividly her lying in the backyard soaking up the hot prairie sun wearing nothing but a starched, white, full body corset; a glass of whiskey in one hand, and a cigarette in the other.

Although I had no idea at the time, years later I learned that her husband had turned her over to the Nazis. He was having an affair with a Dutch woman and wanted his Jewish wife out of the way. My kind-hearted Tante Mina survived Auschwitz, Bergen-Belsen, and Mauthausen, suffered the loss of almost her entire family, and dropped over 100 pounds enduring hard, forced slave labour and near starvation.

The Vittali family lived on the 2nd floor of a canal house. German soldiers had confiscated the 1st floor house beneath, turning it into a local headquarters, and used the 3rd floor house above as a brothel. Constant interruptions, incessant foot-traffic, and inescapable noise were intrusions into the family's daily life.

Jews were forbidden to leave their neighbourhoods, or visit non-Jews. Mina, in defiance of this regulation, secretly visited the Vittali family numerous times. During one such visit, a group of German soldiers was spotted heading towards the house. Terrified that Betje and Giovanni might be discovered and prosecuted for illegally housing a Jew, she declared that when they arrived, she would turn herself in.

In a perceived effort to calm her down, Giovanni put his arm around her shoulder, told her to breathe deeply, and slowly count to three. Mina complied, closed her eyes, and began counting. Before she even reached "two", Giovanni hit her hard on the back of the head, knocking her unconscious. Dragging her into the kitchen's coal shoot, he left her there, out cold, until it was safe to drag her out again.

What saved Mina from the gas chambers was her

arriving alone with no husband or children, under forty-five and therefore able to work, and being a woman of, shall we say, considerable size.

In 1942, Mina Vittali-Tas was stunning and sultry, buxom and shapely. Three years later there was a knock on Betje Vittali's door and there stood a miracle, my mother's favourite aunt. But it was a shocking, barely recognizable skeletal mirage of her. She had no hair, no muscle, no strength. The largest human element left were her hollow eyes, filled with the unseeable. The two women burst into tears, their attempts to speak futile. Everything was already silently known.

Our extended circle of family, formerly numbering over 1200, was reduced to the less than twenty who returned, or were known to have survived, creating a psychological tsunami shock-wave impacting existing and future generations. Like the first sombre tones of a tragic Chopin nocturne, unspeakable pathos overwhelms each new listener.

My mother's story of how Mina ended up in a concentration camp purported that she was so beautiful her husband was afraid she would be "taken advantage of" by soldiers. My cousin, Johannes Vittali, revealed to me a contradictory facet of the story. He has a copy of the police report from an A. Vittali who, on behalf of Mina's husband, Paulus Vittali, reported Mina to the Germans as "missing, not wearing the star, and carrying large amounts of cash,"—all criminal offences for Jews.

Paulus had to have known the Germans would hunt her down and deport her to one of the concentration camps where, he assumed naively, she would be "safe". After all, these were merely supervised "work camps" filled with women and children, old and young, were they not? How bad could they be?

Mina was on the very last transport of Jews out of Westerbork, the same transport carrying Ann Frank, her family, and the other residents of *Het Achterhuis*. On April 15, 1945, she is on record as an inmate of Mauthausen, most likely transported there from Auschwitz in the wave of forced evacuations that occurred in front of advancing Russian troops. On May 5, 1945, American troops liberated the remaining prisoners trapped at Mauthausen, the last operating Nazi concentration camp of WW2. Mina is freed.

The cleaner retelling of Mina's arrest and deportation story is perhaps the one the family preferred. If Sophia Vittali was privy to the darker version, she wasn't going to divulge that to me. Italians protect the family honour.

Mina deserved, at the very least, a tall, frosty glass of whiskey, a slow cigarette, and a long, luxurious corset-clad bath under the Saskatchewan sun.

My mother was absolutely despondent when Mina died in 1991, at the age of ninety-three. She was the only person on earth who shared, guarded, and understood all my mother's secrets. Fabulous Mina. She outlived them all!

After the war, my grandfather, Giovanni Vittali, never spoke to his brother, Paulus, again. When Paulus died in 1975, he bequeathed to his brother a fortune in artwork, furniture, and precious jewellery.

To the great chagrin of my mother, it was all given to the Salvation Army.

*Mina Vittali-Tas, age 60. September 21,
1958.*

DECADES

*A*s a result of my 1978 trip to Holland with my mother, I came to understand that relatives on my maternal side had been arrested, deported, and gassed in concentration camps. What a horrible thing to say out loud, in those exact words. In print, they appear strangely casual, almost normal. Individual, ordinary words, with multiple meanings. Strung together and spoken aloud, they invoke a singular meaning of deeper consequence.

Each of the three houses in Canada that my parents have lived in, two of which I lived in, had some sort of concealed space; out of the way, yet big enough for a person or two. The small door leading to a tiny attic where the Christmas decorations were kept; the crawlspace under a short set of stairs; a narrow basement passageway resembling a pantry. "You could hide in there," my mother would say. Secret annexes. Insurance.

Over the years, and on numerous visits to Victoria, British Columbia, my parent's city of choice for their retirement years, my mother gradually opened up and shared with me what she knew, what she experienced, what she had been told.

My grandmother was the third of nine children. By the war years of 1939 to 1945, all nine were married with families of their own. Extending further down the line were the siblings of their spouses, also married with families.

A partial list of names existed, shown to me once, of those who died in the Holocaust. When did my mother receive this list, and how long ago? Very likely it was given to her by her cousin, Jacob, who could have acquired the information from the Dutch authorities, who would have received it from the Red Cross, who would have discovered it from German documents. The Nazis kept meticulous records.

At the top of the list, her grandfather, her adored Opa, my great-grandfather, Levie Hijman, age seventy-nine. Below him, all eight of his remaining children, their spouses and children, his grandchildren. Each one taken, every life shattered, everyone gone. Somewhere in the middle of the list, a little seven-year-old girl named Stella. I had no idea; she had never been mentioned to me before.

lists upon lists
name after name

unimaginable
unforgivable

In retrospect, it was not hard to surmise why my mother delayed talking about this part of her life to me, to my sister, and never to anyone else outside the family, at least so far as I was aware. Such topics don't drop conveniently into ordinary conversations. Something known, something experienced, something so life-altering, cannot be un-experienced or un-known, and, if shared, the risk of that knowing changes people in unexpected ways.

Odd that she never mentioned any family twins again, though. And by the time I discovered what little I could glean about them, my mother was gone. Between her need for secrecy and my non-conflicting nature, their lives, her involvement with them, what happened to them —shall forever remain unknown. That, in itself, is a tragedy and a regret.

The terror that her secrets would be discovered dominated her life. Between the ages of twelve and seventeen, my mother's necessity of hiding certain truths, whether entrusted or innocently observed and internalized, meant, literally, life or death. If asked, you lied. Children grew up trained to be consummate liars—a habit very hard to break.

Even forty years after our trip to Holland, my mother's index finger still articulated in my direction the admonition of, "Don't you ever tell anyone!"

But why not tell? Was all this secrecy, hiding, and deception a mother's protection, or a woman's fear? Canada was a safe and free country. We grew up completely free and unencumbered. Unlike the German armies, however, Anti-Semitism did not retreat at the end of the 2nd World War.

ON THE VITTALI SIDE, in Amsterdam, lived my mother's beautiful and exotic aunt, Margareta, famous for her ability to predict the future. She was so well known as a psychic that the Nazis attempted to extract predictions from her. She refused. With her undeniable Italian background, there was no fear of reprisal due to her lack of co-operation.

As other-worldly, unbelievable, and even laughable as this may seem, my mother and I both inherited, to some degree, Tante Margareta's predictive abilities.

As a child, Sophia typically spent weekend afternoons with her Opa, Levie Hijman, who lived a few blocks away. One Saturday in 1937, while sitting on the train en route to her weekly visit, she had an overwhelming sense of dread, an unclear vision of something horrible about to happen.

Little Sophia loved her grandfather with all her heart. He spoiled her with peppermints and *zoute dropjes*, and told her she was his favourite. I can imagine him taking all his grandchildren on his knee, one at a time, big brown innocent eyes gazing up adoringly, and him whispering in their ear that they were his favourite, too.

"Hijman eyes," my mother would often reflect, "you have Hijman eyes. And your son, Michael. He has the Hijman eyes."

Her premonition came true as a few short years later, Opa Levie was gone, her aunts and uncles were gone. Cousins her age that she had played with, younger ones she had babysat. Gone. One by one, family by family, they disappeared and never returned.

If my mother had had any other father, a Jewish father, her fate would have been sealed, too. And she knew it.

≈

By the spring of 2013, phone conversations with my mother had undergone an almost imperceptible yet marked evolution. Word by word, minute by minute, talking took on marathon proportions. When forty-five-minute calls stretched into interminable lengths about topics with no definitive relevance and no end in sight, I knew something was wrong. In sheer survival mode, I would put on headphones, turn up my patience meter, and clean the entire house while she talked and talked and talked and talked, as if stopping the "conversation" would prove catastrophic.

One day during such a marathon, Mom said, "Are you talking to me through your computer?"

"Yes," I replied, often using Skype to call her in order to continue carrying on with computer work, uninterrupted.

"You have to stop. People are listening. Bad people. Don't ever call me through your computer again."

Normal discussions no longer existed. Every conversation was punctuated with, "There's someone listening in. Be careful what you say!" Despite gentle attempts to assure her that no illicit listeners were lurking in the background, she became more and more insistent; conversations between mother and daughter now replaced with nonsensical monologues.

My younger sister, Leah, mentioned the possibility of Alzheimer's. That felt rather implausible as Mom's older sister, Christina, was well into her 90s and sharp as a tack. Opa Vittali had lived to eighty-eight, still bossing his sons around in the family construction business in Taree, Australia, to his last day. The paranoia and trauma-centred conversations continued.

In the summer of 2014, my three children, now all in their 30s, along with my two grandsons, the youngest four-months old and the eldest three-and-a-half years old, all converged from Halifax, upstate New York, and Ontario, to Victoria, British Columbia, for a visit with Oma and Opa ter Hart.

My mother was shockingly thin. I was shaken at the deterioration of her mental and physical state. Although he tried his very best, my father—unable, unwilling, or a bit of both—had no idea how to cope with the changes happening to his wife. He sat watching sports and news most of the day while she lay, zombie-like, sweltering in her bed. When together in the living room, they sat in absolute silence; my mother staring, my father reading. The ticking of the family Delft tiled Dutch wall clock almost deafening as it insistently marked off the minutes of their lives.

Mom rallied upon our arrival and gave a fantastic show of remembering all of us. She held her chubby-faced little great-grandson for the first time, cooing and making faces at him, and delighting in his baby belly laugh. She asked her grandchildren all the right questions about university, jobs, relationships, and said over and over how wonderful it was to see them. As is all too common in similar scenes enacted in bedrooms, nursing, and care homes in every society, it was to be the last time.

At the end of the visit, everyone departed on schedule, returning to their own lives and familiar routines. Such is the inevitability of life's trajectory. Young people rush into their futures while parents and grandparents, locked in the past, can do little but watch them go, waving in spirit until they cannot see them anymore.

The decision for me to stay required zero thought. Dad needed support and Mom needed constant care. Delaying my return ticket for three weeks, I was happy to cook, clean, and care for my mother, and be a conversational companion to my father.

I rarely left the house except to indulge in a private walk each evening. Leaving their well-groomed Victoria neighbourhood, I short-cutted and zig-zagged my way through side streets and hidden walkways down to the Pacific Ocean. My only compatriots the domesticated deer as they patrolled streets and groomed lawns, their enormous eyes gazing at me non-plussed as I passed. Driftwood serving as seating, I hung out on the rough beach taking in the calm rhythm of the waves, their pulse clearing my head before heading back up again.

Once, while in my mother's room working on my laptop and seated in the chair beside her bed, she appeared to be asleep—hands folded and still, breathing barely audible. I glanced over and caught her peeking at me, one brown eye open to catch what I was doing. It quickly shuttered as she stealthily fell back to "being asleep." There was a spark of mental sharpness in her yet.

"She's always loved being fussed over," Dad commented, following me around as I carried on my new daily role as nurse, beautician, and chef.

Of course she did. In her youth, the renowned beauty of the Vittali family enjoyed an endless trail of male admirers to dote on her. She even had her own personal maid and housekeeper as a company perk when she was the secretary for the Dutch Ambassador. Before marrying, Sophia travelled the world in her secretarial position, and lived in Amsterdam, Rome, Sydney, Ottawa, and Paris. In her off hours, she was an actress of some renown, an activity she dearly loved, and one she continued to pursue her entire life.

Jan ter Hart adored his enchanting wife, with her

black hair and white skin reminiscent of Snow White. Summertime always saw my mother sheltered by wide-brimmed hats, staving off freckles and a tan at all costs. Somehow, he scrimped on his own basics in order to shower her with diamonds, fur coats, pearls, hand-crafted gold necklaces, and gem-studded bracelets. Quite impressive for the tall, handsome, blue-eyed, adventurous sailor who immigrated to Canada with $121 in his pocket. His daughters now treasure these treasures.

Leaving his career as a Dutch merchant ship's officer, Jan earned his land surveyor's certificate and moved to Saskatchewan, which had plenty of land to survey, in 1955. Not much opportunity for showcasing Christian Dior gowns, but a sparkle of diamond now and then helped Sophia forget how far away Saskatchewan was from the rest of the world.

MY THREE WEEKS WAS UP. The inevitable time came for me to leave Victoria. My poor mother, disappointment sadly evident, sat still and expressionless in her chair. As a buffer and welcome relief, she had enjoyed having someone answer her little ringing bell, cook all the meals, encourage gentle exercises, change support stockings, be a bathroom buddy, pluck chin hairs. You name it. I did it. She liked it.

When her mother became ill, Sophia travelled with her firstborn son, baby Jantje, from Saskatoon to Taree, Australia. She stayed — caring, cleaning, cooking — for six months until her mother died, six days before her daughter's twenty-ninth birthday. Perhaps the same was expected of me.

My grandmother contracted cervical cancer. She was

forced to endure irradiation by the Nazis, who used radiation as a means of mandatory sterilization for mixed-marriage Jewish women of childbearing age. Considering she was fifty-four at the time, sterilization was ridiculously unnecessary. Although Betje Vittali-Hijman, unlike all her siblings, was spared deportation to a concentration camp, her life was still taken by the Nazis.

Dad, eminently practical, insisted I return to my own life.

A few years earlier, my husband and I had re-located from Bobcaygeon, Ontario to just north of Kingston, Ontario. We purchased a farm with an abandoned old heritage apple orchard and rambling ranch-style farmhouse. The day we moved in, May 14, 2014, I discovered a forsaken vegetable garden on the property displaying a few random asparagus spears shooting up, and one lone, red tulip bulb in bloom.

Tulips are my soul flower. I must have planted over 1,000 of them from Estevan to Calgary to Saint John to Bobcaygeon to Kingston; a blaze of colour left behind for others to enjoy. As each hard bulb is buried deep in the cold November ground, I revel in my power to shape the destiny of that tiny corner of my future. Bulbs are eternal hope; a promise that life can still flourish from that which appears dead.

My Dutch ancestors also had an ongoing relationship with tulips. They bought them, traded them, planted them, delighted in them. And, as a measure of last resort, ate them.

Because of my being away at a crucial time for our orchard, we lost most of the crop that summer to the voracious apple maggot fly. I never let on. The future held more apples; it did not hold another mother.

LIBERATION!

remendous joy and exhilaration greet the liberation of Holland, free at last from an oppressive five-year reign of subjugation. May 5, 1945. General Charles Foulkes, Commander of the 1st Canadian Corps, accepts the surrender of the occupying German forces.

Canadian soldiers are treated like heroes. Thousands of Dutch citizens throng the streets, greeting these young men with outbursts of appreciation as the soldiers move from town to town, city to city, bringing much needed supplies and relief to a beleaguered and starving people.

The day the Canadians liberate Amsterdam, Sophia Vittali is seventeen years old. After suffering through the long, hard Hunger Winter of 1945, she is wearing clothes too small on a body too thin. Their family diet, reduced to tulip bulbs and beets, has wasted her away. They were the lucky ones; starvation stood at their door but never fully entered in.

Her mother hands her the inconceivable — a chocolate bar — secretly stashed for years in some hidden cupboard, waiting auspiciously for this hoped-for day. Smiling, friendly soldiers overtake the streets of Amsterdam and the crowd, wild with the dizziness of freedom, is drunk with joy.

Sophia joins the exuberant crowd, pushing and elbowing her way to the front of the throng. She thrusts out her small yet monumental sacrifice to a young man in uniform with a strange, never before heard foreign accent. He grins at her and tips his hat.

Meanwhile, from somewhere inside the same crowd, Jan ter Hart Junior clambers up a streetlight pole, hangs precariously off the side, head thrust forward with unbridled excitement, and watches the Canadians, many not much older than he, ride by in trucks and jeeps, waving, cheering, celebrating.

CANADA not only sheltered the Dutch Royal family in exile, its soldiers also rescued the people of the Netherlands from their oppressors. A strong bond, almost a type of love, has existed between Canada and Holland ever since. My family is a veritable personification of this bond.

My father is the young man in the photo dangling off the lower right hand side of the streetlight pole, his head leaning forward over the crowd.

Holland gradually set mourning aside and abandoned its war shroud. As each day went by, friends, family, and neighbours watched and waited. Some souls returned, solitary, burdened with truths not to be believed and miseries not to be imagined. But none returned from the Levie Hijman line ... father, brothers, sisters, aunts, uncles, spouses, nieces, nephews, cousins ... no one.

Levie's wife, Rachel, my great-grandmother, died in 1931 at the age of sixty-eight when my mother was only four years old. A crushing loss at the time, her death would prove to be fortuitous, saving her from witnessing the suffering of her babies, their babies, and their babies.

Of the entire Dutch Jewish population, 75 to 80% were killed between 1941 and 1944, the highest statistic in all of Europe. My great-grandmother was mercifully spared the trauma of witnessing and experiencing this inexplicable horror.

Sophia Maria Vittali, age 17. Amsterdam, 1944.

2015 - VICTORIA

ALTERED

*B*y the summer of 2015, my father tragically resembled the proverbial frog sitting in a pot of water on the stove, unaware that someone had turned the heat on, and that things were about to boil over. The frailty and mental shutdown that had overtaken his wife paralyzed him. Old age had arrived, uninvited. It moved in and decided to stay.

I came for another ten-day visit, but this time realized almost immediately that not only did I need to extend my stay, I needed to remain with my parents until we could place my mother into a complex-care facility.

My mother had always had a dynamic personality. She ruled relationships, dominated our family, competently oversaw and even governed various cultural and community associations. Now she could not get herself to the bathroom in time, anytime. Discreetly, I cleaned up after her and threw out the rug.

Dad grumbled that he could not understand why she didn't just get up and do the things she always did and had been doing for the almost sixty years of their marriage. She wouldn't eat, was incapable of cooking, and lost any ability to accomplish the smallest task or make any decision. He had no understanding of, and seemed thoroughly confused by, mental illness. Coming from a long line of strong, stalwart and sharp-minded ancestors, it was out of his range of experience.

In my younger years, I too often overheard occasional adult comments about elderly people "who had lost it". I can't imagine the comments were intentionally unkind, but they never came out sounding right. "Remember Mrs. Carlson? She's lost it, you know. Doesn't recognize anyone anymore." As if, somehow, it was Mrs. Carlson's or whoever's, fault, and they should have tried harder not to lose it, whatever "it" was.

EARLY IN THE WAR, the ter Hart family was ordered out of their large brick home located on an island in the Amsterdam inner harbour. Due to its strategic location, the Nazis turned the home into a headquarters for that area. The displaced family of four moved into the home of a recently deported Jewish family, the canal house adjoining my mother's.

In 1940, my parents were both thirteen years old. Although the German occupation of Holland would steal their formative years, they *were* still teenagers!

Sophia, in an attempt to catch the attention of young Jan, the new, blonde-haired, blue-eyed boy living next door, went over one day to practice her violin, having enlisted his sister, Zulma, to accompany her on the piano. It was apparently quite awful as the intended audience crawled out a second-floor side window and escaped to the roof to give his ears a break from the musical chaos below.

After the war, the two followed different paths: Jan, the life of a merchant ship's officer and Sophia, a career in government. But love cannot be denied. The two married in Paris on January 12, 1956, my mother glamorous and ravishing in a deep emerald green, velvet and taffeta Christian Dior gown, her jet-black hair styled à la Audrey Hepburn. Three weeks later she found herself in Regina, Saskatchewan, in the dead cold of an endless Canadian winter.

A single survivor of the Jewish family formerly living in my father's house returned, alone. It had been their house, their home, their life. My grandfather stood and looked at him in the doorway and said, "What do you want me to do? Put my family out on the street?" The man asked to come inside, just for a moment. Opa, hesitating, allowed him in.

Walking straight upstairs to one of the bedrooms, he pried up a floorboard to retrieve a box, its contents unknown, hidden, literally, underfoot the entire time, unbeknownst to anyone but himself. After a moment, he retreated down the stairs, the remnants of a former life under his arm, was shown the door, then gone.

This scene repeated itself over and over again for those very few who did, somehow, return. They no longer had homes, possessions, money, jobs, a way of life, or barely even themselves. As people were brutalized, so also were their possessions: looted, stolen, destroyed, taken over, or burned. Men and women fought to survive against unfathomable odds driven by perhaps the most significant motivating factor alive, the desire to return home, only to discover there was no more home. Survivors finding their way back were met with suspicion, a certain level of annoyance, distrust and indifference, and were completely and utterly displaced. It wasn't just the Nazis who indulged in heinous behaviour.

Once, during her last days at home, my mother asked me to retrieve a small box of antique jewellery, trinkets, and gold watches hidden deep inside her bathroom linen closet. Upon opening, she fingered the items for a while, each one fondled and viewed with care, a faraway look in her eye. After a few minutes, she closed the lid and held out the nondescript box for me to bury again.

The aftermath of war can be as hard to bear as war itself.

My mother was hospitalized for some time while they attempted to determine her specific variety of Alzheimer's, if that was indeed what she had. The eventual diagnosis was Lewy body dementia, the symptoms of which include:

- changes in thinking and reasoning
- confusion and alertness that varies significantly from one time of day to another or from one day to the next
- slowness, gait imbalance and other Parkinsonian movement features
- well-formed visual hallucinations
- delusions
- trouble interpreting visual information
- sleep disturbances
- malfunctions of the autonomic nervous system

- memory loss, possibly significant, but less
  prominent than in Alzheimer's

The above described my mother exactly, except for memory loss; many memories, too many. Paranoia plagued her. During one hospital visit she looked over at me, wide-eyed. "That's not Stella. It looks like Stella, but Stella would never wear such dirty clothes. This must be someone pretending to be Stella."

Hands jerking anxiously in the air, she flailed away at imaginary cobwebs drifting down from the hospital ceiling. Crystal clear memories were of the far distant past rather than the present; a horrible, haunting past which refused to leave, and robbed her of any peace. She had terrifying hallucinations. Nazis were crawling through the hospital windows, ready to torture any and all secrets out of her. An ambulance siren's distant wail sent her into hysterics, her frail conscience convinced that bombs would follow at any minute.

Both my parents frequently talked about the "whistle" that accompanied falling bombs. If you heard it, the bomb was destined to fall on your neighbour, not you. If silent, it was directly above, and you may not live to crawl out from under the devastation.

In desperation at the thought of being discovered by her imaginary Nazi abusers, she cried out about how she knew *where everything was*, that *millions of dollars were at stake*, and, if discovered, *it would be the biggest breaking news story of all time*.

Strange thing about secrets; if you harbour one, it can bring either power or panic into your life.

Years earlier, she disclosed to me how Jewish friends and neighbours brought money, gold, diamonds, jewellery, and other valuables in secret to the house on the Amsteldijk. In confidence and despair, they begged my grandfather, a trusted and well-established building contractor, to "take care" of their valuables for them.

My mother's youngest brother, wild and crazy, loveable Uncle Joe corroborated this story. I met him for the first time when my husband and I travelled to Australia in late August 2017 to celebrate my Tante Christina's 100th birthday on September 6, 2017.

There is very likely a WW2 fortune buried under the streets and buildings of Amsterdam, hidden by the GA Vittali Building and Construction Company.

My grandfather, Giovanni Antonio Vittali,
sporting a hat, his hands by his side, stands
on the scaffold, furthest left. Amsterdam,
1948.

The medication prescribed for my mother to control
her dementia removed her hallucinations and delusions,
removed her terror and nightmares, and removed her
personality.

On her return home from the hospital, she barely

spoke, and when she did, her responses were monosyllabic. She no longer smiled, no longer interacted even remotely effectively, and ate no more than a mouthful at mealtimes. Moving my mother from her bed to her chair and back again was a Herculean feat. Any desire to do or achieve had completely evaporated. She was 103 pounds whereas, in her healthier years, she had been a substantial size eighteen. I incorporated extra amounts of margarine and mayonnaise into her food in a last-ditch effort to put a little weight on her. Even a personalized menu of her favourite foods could not entice her: pickled beets with onions, salted herring on crackers, soft-boiled eggs on toast, and Dutch croquettes from the baker downtown.

Life was interminably dull. One evening, while looking for something, anything, to entertain her, I discovered *La Bohème* playing on CBC Radio One. She adored music and loved opera in particular. Her face began to soften and relax. She smiled—the familiar music helping her forget where, who, and what she was as strains of *"Sì, mi chia mano Mimì"* floated around her.

For a moment, she is again a head-turning black-haired beauty, seated in luxurious elegance at the opera house in Amsterdam, exquisite in a burgundy satin gown and carried away on wings of song.

My mother's health evolved into an increasingly impossible situation. Leah and I colluded to convince Dad that Mom needed to be in a complex-care facility. Our mutual plotting was transparent and short-lived. He needed little convincing.

After interminable days of visiting almost every single complex-care facility available in Victoria, the veritable utopia of elderly housing, we found an opening for her at St. Charles Manor.

In the early morning of August 8, 2015, Sophia ter

Hart, née Vittali, was carried downstairs on a stretcher out of her home of thirty-one years, and transported by ambulance across town. I rode along, perched beside her, while her husband and youngest daughter followed by car behind. Together we moved our beautiful, larger-than-life mother into her new home — now a tiny woman in a tiny room whose life had shrunk to this.

Strange how the abnormal morphs into the new normal with such casualness. Attentive but detached personal workers pressed a monotonous routine on each day, adhering to a set time schedule, whether natural to those under their care or not.

My father, diligently and without fail, visited his teenage sweetheart daily. This usually involved him falling asleep in her room, slumped in the only available chair while she lay stone-like in bed, staring at the ceiling. A large window offered a reasonable view of the home's back garden, green and lush, yet her blank eyes seemed to focus only on the flat-white ceiling. But her husband was there, and that was important.

Sometimes she would talk incessantly about nothing, and other times be completely "on the ball". In one of her rare and most lucid moments while still in the hospital, she looked at both my sister and me and stated, "So many lies. I have told so many lies. How can I ever be forgiven?" I'll never forget her tortured expression of complete awareness.

It was difficult to know what to expect. After a few weeks, she was given new medications, which thankfully helped, and allowed her to be a version of herself most of the time.

Leah, ever present and ever faithful, did her best to bring cheer and humour into every visit with Janner, her adorable little blonde toddler in tow, holding his baby arms up to his grandmother with a heartbreaking, "I love you Oma."

I called at least three times a week, every week, and had the same conversation with her each time. I don't think she ever remembered. "Hey Dad, did Mom mention I called?" A sadly rhetorical question.

"No, I don't think so. No, she didn't," not an unexpected reply.

Once my mother commented that people trying to go into hiding had to choose between children. You could hide one, maybe two, but not four. "I would choose Bert and Leah," a startling and revealing comment that blindsided me. "You and Jantje would be fine on your own."

- **Jantje** *(little Jan)*: clever, funny, aloof, successful, independent
- **Bert**: brilliant yet fragile, temperamental, moody, eccentric
- **Stella**: quietly stubborn, determined, patient, free-spirited
- **Leah**: fun-loving, big-hearted, generous, reactive, vulnerable

As sharp as the words were, she was right.

January 12, 2016
Jan and Sophia ter Hart
60th Wedding Anniversary

Mom expressed to Leah and I how much she would love a fancy *Come and Go Tea* in honour of the occasion.

She adored parties and holidays, openly jealous when friends lucky enough to have family nearby would throw big shindigs for special days and events.

My sister and I set to planning. Leah booked the fellowship hall at the Gordon Head United Church, which my parents had attended for years. Our parent's house veritably rattled with teacups and china. There was no shortage of those. The menu was to comprise an assortment of elegant sandwiches, sweet pickles, olives, various nibblies, and delectable dainties.

To-Do List:

- guest list composed
- long-time friends invited
- airplane tickets booked

Would I entertain the residents at St. Charles on the ancient-of-days upright piano when I arrived? Of course. It would be a welcome break from the well-meaning guitar player who showed up every Wednesday afternoon and played the identical set of songs ... every ... single ... time.

The date of the Anniversary Tea was finalized for January 16, 2016, from 2:00 p.m. to 4:00 p.m., a few days after the actual anniversary date, the weekend being more convenient for all.

January 14, 2016
Itinerary:

Kingston to Toronto, Toronto to Calgary, Calgary to Vancouver, Vancouver to Victoria

For no reason whatsoever, my flight from Toronto to Calgary is nonchalantly late. I am highly anxious about my connecting flight, so I ask the attendant repeatedly if I have sufficient time to connect, only to be told that the connecting flight crew is fully aware, and to please stop worrying.

Stuck towards the back of the plane, when we finally do land, I disembark as fast as I can and rush to the connecting gate. My heart sinks to find the departure area for the Calgary to Vancouver connection vacated with not a soul in sight, even though the flight is not set to leave for another fifteen minutes. I can literally see the plane sitting on the tarmac.

I run back to the Toronto arrival gate, frantically ask why there is no one at my departure gate, and how can I board the Calgary flight.

"We cannot let you on the plane. Your luggage is unable to be put on the plane at this time. Regulations require you to travel with your luggage."

An expressionless face barely looks up as he drones out his obligatory response.

I miss the Calgary to Vancouver connection and was ragingly, furiously angry. I could do nothing but sit and steam, pace and wait.

It was 11:30 p.m. when I finally arrived, instead of my originally scheduled 8:00 p.m. arrival. I could have seen my mother that night. I could have spoken with her. I could have sat with her, held her hand, combed her hair, put moisturizer on her face.

A frantic phone call from my sister wakes me up the next morning, her previous attempts much earlier failing to penetrate my deep sleep down in the basement bedroom. Mom has suffered a massive stroke and is at the hospital. Barely awake, Dad hears the tone of the conversation and shuffles down the hall to see what is going on. His face falls at the news; his head drops into his hands. A few familiar Dutch words escape. We brace ourselves and head out.

A short time after we arrive at the Royal Jubilee Hospital, orderlies move our mother from Emergency to Hospice, her stroke so severe there is nothing the doctor can do, nothing any of us can do but wait for the inevitable.

Our older brothers arrive from Edmonton and Vancouver; Jan by plane and Bert via sailboat, a trip of some four hours from the mainland to Victoria. We keep telling Mom that Bert will be here soon, that he is on his way.

Each stands vigil. Each takes a turn with the various comings and goings as are still required. Jantje, a brilliantly successful criminal lawyer, sets up a makeshift workspace using the rolling bed tray as a desk in a corner of Mom's room. He hands his credit card over to Leah, and off we go to buy whatever we can find in the hospital to keep everyone fed.

One by one, invited wedding anniversary tea guests are called. Somehow, there is little surprise in their voices at the news. Young people talk about their weekends. Old people talk about hip replacements and which memorial service luncheons to attend.

The groom of sixty years gently presents his bride

with the diamond bracelet he had so thoughtfully purchased for their sixtieth wedding anniversary, fastening it softly around her emaciated wrist, the skin dry and thin. One last gift of glitter. "This is for you, Fietje, my darling, my life."

I had packed no piano books—a conscious decision— a premonition that there would be no music.

GOOGLED

$\mathcal{A}$fter my mother died, Dad, age eight-eight, came to stay with us in May that same year. Worry-free days of leisure followed; Dad languidly reading Louis L'Amour novels, fishing for wide-mouth bass and sunfish in Loughborough Lake, feeding the goldfish in our pond, and sitting outside with no shirt on, enjoying an early start to a hot, humid Ontario summer. He took it upon himself to wash the dishes, a genetic trait perhaps.

Although he possessed a superhuman ability to fix and repair anything broken or not functioning, he had few skills as a cook. However, he could perform a spectacular breakfast routine.

The procedure is as follows:

- Bring a medium-sized pot of water to a slight boil.
- Add one egg, boil one minute then turn off heat and let sit for five minutes; set table.

- Remove egg with slotted spoon and place in egg cup to cool.
- Scoop one ladle of hot egg water into bowl containing one tablespoon oatmeal and one tablespoon cream of wheat. Put in microwave for sixty seconds.
- Scoop one ladle of hot egg water into coffee mug.
- Add one teaspoon instant coffee, one teaspoon sugar and a splash of milk.
- Make toast with bread from the 50% off bin at Walmart.
- Sit down to a delicious, homemade breakfast.
- Wash dishes in pot of remaining hot egg water.
- Leave water in pot for later use.

Thrift. Save where you can, use what you have, then do without, regardless of any urgency.

The Dutch drop everything for coffee and cookies at 11:00 a.m. and snacks at 4:00 p.m. At the ready in my kitchen, copious amounts of freshly baked goodies complete with mountains of whipped cream, a pantry staple. Time passed munching cookies, reminiscing about life in Saskatchewan, so carefree and easy in the 1960s and '70s, and laughing about the innocent fun we created for ourselves with whatever resources we could find.

After the liberation of Holland and the ending of WW2, my father, like his father before him, chose a life at sea. He took on a position with various Dutch merchant cargo ship companies delivering huge shipments of goods to ports around the world. "Hey Dad, let's see if we can find some of those ships." He dictated. I Googled.

Every vessel he had ever served on miraculously appeared via a simple internet search. Memories and astonishment now occupied the same space at the kitchen table. After leaving his sailing days behind to marry my mother and move to Canada, Jan ter Hart had had no opportunity to revisit that part of his life. But now— BINGO—here he was, gawking at multiple photos of huge freighters appearing right before his eyes, straight out of 1947.

"Look there—right there—I can't believe it—that's the window of the cabin I slept in!" An emphatic index finger jabbing and indicating exact spots. "I stood on THAT deck during my watch. My father was the chief engineer on THAT ship." How exhilarating to have discovered this new world way into a past world life. Blue eyes wide and alert and shoulders pressed forward, he eagerly anticipated the next miracle to materialize on my laptop.

Google discovered the ter Hart family home in the Amsterdam harbour, the one confiscated by the Nazis, and bombed to the ground by the allies. "Incredible!" He was almost overwhelmed by this unexpected hurtling into his childhood. "My room was there, in that upper corner on the second floor overlooking the ocean. Unbelievable! That's where I used to go fishing, right on that point every day after school,"—more definitive tapping on the black-and-white photograph on the screen—"and that's my father's office, and there's my mother's kitchen."

In fifty-six years, it never occurred to me to ask, so I took advantage of the moment. "Do you know much about your father's parents, your Opa and Oma?" It seemed a casual, normal question for a child to ask of a parent, at any age.

My assumptions of normal possible responses—old age, diabetes, heart attacks—were shattered by the actual response, "No, I never knew them. My father, before I was born, arrived home from being away at sea for over a year to discover both his parents dead."

"What? Really?!" My ecstatic mood of discovery dissipating into inexorable sadness. "When, what year? What happened?"

"I have no idea."

Dad—circumspect over his failure to ask. Me— determined to find out.

∾

June 12, 2016

Dear Stella,
Free trial

This is a brief update that your 14-day free trial for an annual data subscription has started. You now have unlimited access to billions of historical records! Feel free to visit MyHeritage SuperSearch and search for your ancestors. At the end of the trial period, you will be charged US $119.40 for one year of access. You can review your subscriptions and take action anytime on your Account > My Purchases page.

Record Matching. As a data customer you enjoy full access to our Record Matching Technology at no additional cost. This is an extremely powerful feature that automatically finds historical records relevant to your family tree. For this purpose, we have created a free, private family site for you on MyHeritage. It is currently empty.

By creating your family tree on your family site using our

friendly tools, or importing your existing GEDCOM file, you will automatically receive your Record Matches for free. Learn more about Record Matches and see the praise this technology received from some of the world's foremost genealogists.

HISTORY HAS ALWAYS BEEN a welcome companion to me. Growing up, I buried myself in biographies, autobiographies, and historical fiction. Most nine-year-old girls in my Grade 3 class dreamed of ballerinas and movie stars; I imagined myself an archeologist. For a career, I studied Musicology and became a Royal Conservatory of Toronto music history examiner. Digging into the past was right up my alley.

My new geneology hobby quickly morphed into an obsession. I poured hours plugging in this name and that name, the rhythmic ticking of our Dutch clock on the living room wall accompanying me, its brass horse and rider pendulum keeping pace with my findings. Every obscure relative uncovered was added into our family tree, their dates and details authenticated against matching records automatically popping up in my genealogy account.

I hunted down the mysterious dates of the lives of my great-grandparents, the ones that died while their thirty-eight-year-old only son was at sea.

Jan Daniel ter Hart
Great-grandfather
Mar 30 1862 - Dec 31 1924

Maria Alida Hissink (ter Hart)

Great-grandmother
Oct 22 1862 - Jan 11 1925

What happened? There was no longer anyone alive who might know. Their dates gave no answers, only clues.

A first theory considered the Spanish Flu Epidemic, but the dates were off, that epidemic having run its course through Europe by the end of 1919. The next devastating illness to sweep the country was malaria, which raged through post WW1 Europe, and peaked between 1922 and 1925. It is entirely plausible that Jan Daniel ter Hart contracted malaria, which killed him, followed by Maria Alida, eleven days later. Husband, then wife—the "cared-for" and the "care-giver"—both were sixty-two.

My grandfather surely sought out whatever news he could about his parents, but he did not share that with my dad, who never thought to ask. But then, Father never quite forgave Son for abandoning war-ravaged Holland and immigrating to Canada at a time when Holland needed their young people the most.

The aristocratic Family ter Hart lived in the Netherlands for over 700 years, and I still have many relatives living there. The House ter Hart boasted its own castle, its existence and strategic location mentioned in various Dutch historical records. Today, a modest modern day monument marks its location in the town of *Halfweg*, meaning literally "half way," located between Haarlem and Amsterdam.

❧

ON OCTOBER 26, 2019, my brother, Bert, sailed out of the Victoria, British Columbia harbour in his forty-foot ocean-faring sailboat to circumnavigate the globe, non-stop, and with no electronic devices of any kind to guide him, a North American first.

In the midst of his voyage, the coronavirus, COVID-19, swept over the globe, including Canada and the Netherlands, thrusting my brother into the rare position of being possibly the safest person on the planet.

The proposed six-month journey elongated into 270 days of gruelling weather, physical endurance to the point of starvation and exhaustion, and debilitating emptiness. But he survived and succeeded!

Upon returning to port, ninety-two-year-old Jan Daniel ter Hart, alive and well, stood on the shore, ready to greet his son—a very different homecoming experience than the former Jan Daniel, ninety-four years ago.

ALL THOSE NEBULOUS ter Hart relatives I had met in Holland in 1978, many now gone, received a final, loving placement on the appropriate tree branch, memories of them filling my mind.

The paternal side burgeoned past 600 individuals, dates and places uncovering migrations of Huguenot ancestors into Holland from my father's maternal side, fleeing religious persecution in France.

In stark contrast, my mother's maternal side, despite weeks of genealogy gazing, was virtually empty. I did not, however, find this at all unusual, or unexpected, given what I knew about the loss of the Hijman family during the war.

Months into my research, an unknown My Heritage member confirmed various Italian family members on my maternal, paternal side. "Well, would you look at that—

it's Opa and Oma Vittali!" I had previously entered my grandparent's information, but with only the barest of details. Here appeared new people, with birthdates, birthplaces, marriages, residences, and occupations. "My mother! And Tante Christina, Uncle Tony, and Uncle Joe. But ... who are all these others?"

Clicking on the link for Giovanni Vittali unleashed a flood of Italian relatives with names repeating for generations — Pietro, Antonio, Giuseppe, Giovanni, Sophia, Margareta, Maria, Christina — tracing all the way back to the 1400s in Italy. I marvelled at this wealth of unfolding family history.

How the first Vittali wound up in a cold, adopted northern country is one of our family's dramatic sagas. At the age of sixteen, Pietro Antonio, enraged with his father over some unknown disagreement, stormed out the door of his home in Druogno, Italy, the despairing wails of his mother and loud shouts, fist shakings, and exclamations of his father trailing long after him.

Young Pietro trudged north, leaving Italy and continuing through Switzerland until his anger was all walked out, and he found himself in Amsterdam, Holland. Teenagers will be teenagers, whether it be the year 1808 or 2021.

And here he was. My great-great-GREAT-grandfather, waving at me through the dash between his dates.

REVELATION

I never expected to find what I found, or how I found it. Facing something standing squarely in front of you forces a stronger reaction than the mere absent awareness of it.

One by one, the brothers and sisters of my grandmother, Elisabeth (Betje) Vittali-Hijman, along with their spouses, children, and grandchildren, popped up as genealogical Record Matches.

This time, however, everything was different. Not the normalcy of dates with associated towns of birth and cities of residence followed by long, growing into old-age gaps of seventy, eighty-plus years. No. In front of my eyes —places—horrible places—places branded with a level of cruel hatred unequalled in human history: Auschwitz, Sobibor, Mauthausen, Bergen-Belsen, Westerbork. Over and over and over again. And dates—appalling dates— end-of-life dates of mothers with children, husbands and wives, siblings and grandparents—all on the same date.

Here they were: my mother's playmate cousins who teased her, the uncles who scowled and told her to be quiet, embarrassed everyone with bad jokes on birthdays and drank too much on holidays, the aunts who gave thoughtful presents and dried her tears, her much-loved grandfather. All of them. Gone.

It was a stunning moment of awareness and grief. This was so far beyond my mother's list.

Shocked, I stared at the dates and places. The realization of the meaning behind them dropped heavily around me, stripping away all ownership of the present and shoving me into a terrible past. With a tremendous sense of obligation coupled with deep respect, I quietly, gently, soberly, confirmed all of their information into our family tree.

I wondered how my mother would feel if she knew what I was doing. Here I was, pouring myself into excavating everything she had spent her life burying. No secret is safe forever.

Our maternal branch began to grow and grow and grow.

PLEASANTDALE SUBDIVISION, built in the early 1960s from lots surveyed by my father, supported two schools side by side, an expansive wildflower field separating them. North of Pleasantdale Public School, which my siblings and I attended, standing witness to harsh pioneer beginnings was the Estevan cemetery, placed high on a wind-swept grassy hill. Facing east, across a broad expanse of flat prairie, was this other school. Children played outside at recess, just like us. They walked to this other school, just like us. As I stood in my school's playground and watched from afar, I often wondered about its purpose, this other school, this twin of my own school.

"That's a Catholic school." My mother answered my question, but her answer didn't answer my question. "It's called Sacred Heart." Pleasantdale. Sacred Heart. Such soothing names. How was I to know what Catholic meant? Maybe they kept plastic on their new furniture, too.

Brownies gathered on Tuesdays after school, and I was going to be one, a Brownie, now that I was old enough to join. The concept of earning badges and rewards for accomplishing tasks was enticingly fantastic. I ate up tests, games, and challenges! The newly formed Brownie troop met at Sacred Heart School. Imagine! I was going to be inside the Sacred Heart.

After two months of *ta-whit ta-whooing* and badge-chasing, a Brownie Halloween party was planned. October 31st each year presented one of two themes for me: Little Red Riding Hood or The Little Dutch Girl. I once attempted to break with tradition by creating a tree costume out of tubes of construction paper and generous amounts of tape accompanied by copious stapling. A royal fail, so back to the old standbys, this year falling to The Little Dutch Girl.

After school on the much-anticipated day, across the open field I went, tromping about in real wooden shoes, dressed and ready to enjoy the festivities. The option to walk on the sidewalk like a normal person existed, safe at the edge of Dieppe Crescent, but bravery to face the unknown was expected during Halloween, so I chose uncharted open territory. My outstretched hand brushed the tops of dried, tender wildflower blossoms as I traipsed along, their summer glory long relinquished.

Once inside, I noticed a new girl standing off by

herself against the gym wall. She sported no fanciful or scary outfit or weird makeup. She was just a little girl, looking lost. The Brownie leader made her step forward and introduced her to the motley bevy of initiated girls staring back at her, all sporting various homemade outfits skillfully sewn on knee-powered Singer sewing machines by stay-at-home housewives.

Her name was Debbie. What a dreamy name. I wished my birth had imbued upon me such a lovely, popular name. I detested "Stella". So ponderous ... oppressive ... old.

Every girl around me trilled sweet, light names like Carol, Nancy, and Tammy. What did my name elicit? Teasing and torture. Boys chasing me, laughing and yelling "Smella Terrible Fart" and cruel Grade 6 girls chanting "Stella has a Fella". My only defence strategy? Scream my entire Dutch repertoire of insults at them, mostly two main phrases: *ben je helemaal gek* and my brothers' personal favourite, *blote billen gezicht*. Even hurtling out *Wil je een kopje thee!?* at the top of one's lungs transforms an otherwise innocuous request into a seemingly dangerous threat.

Once, as a young teenager, I asked my mother what my name, Stella Claire, meant. The response necessitated a resultant change of attitude. "Star Bright, which is how I imagine my mother to be, a star in the heavens looking down on all of us."

The only other Stella in Estevan was a cow. Not a person, but an actual, real cow. I met said cow once, an event occurring at the same time of my being made aware of her nomenclature. She had lovely eyes.

Debbie had not been told about the Halloween party. Her face betrayed the pain of standing out, and any desperate hope for sudden invisibility futile. A few of the bigger girls teased and laughed, making fun of her regular clothes. Visibly hurt, like an injured bird, she was defenceless in the face of these grinning cats.

So, I shared my costume with her. Off came the embroidered white cotton apron that layered over my long, full-length, heavy Dutch wool skirt with its multicoloured vertical stripes, and around her waist it went. Fortunately, both of us were the same size. Next off, my lace Dutch winged cap, its white satin ribbons forming a dainty bow under her chin. Now, we each resembled Little Dutch Girls, she more so than I, with her blonde hair versus my dark locks. Well, close enough to pass for that afternoon, anyway.

The following week at Brownies, I waited for her, my new friend. Time passed. Was she late, or forgot, or quit? I asked one of the leaders, volunteers bestowed with the titles of Tawny Owl and Brown Owl, if Debbie was going to be coming back again. "No, I'm afraid not. Debbie and her family were all killed in a car accident last weekend."

I was seven years old. The words slapped me hard across the face. While still standing, with my little self paralyzed to a designated spot on the gym floor, Tawny Owl turned to Brown Owl and described how the father's head had been cut off by the broken windshield when he was thrown from the car.

There I was, face to face with the stark realization of the ever-present possibility of unforeseen human tragedy and death, and human callousness. It was an all-defining, maturing moment. Nightmares ensued. Brownie meetings were never the same.

I didn't tell anyone about Debbie and the Dutch Girl costume. Kindness in the face of cruelty, and standing up to something bigger, was, and felt at the time, ordinary, not praiseworthy. My actions were reactions. But I have never forgotten the magnitude of understanding that I had done what was right, and given joy to another, if only for a moment, before eternity.

How grievous that humans, generally, still seem unable to evolve beyond being the hunter, the hunted, or the watcher.

OH MY GOD

Staring at me from my genealogy line.
A set of Holocaust twins.
Auschwitz. Murdered.

WAR

1940 - *INCONCEIVABLE*

*I*t was an unsettling New Year's Eve. Joel's distracted gaze took in his wife's family—four older sisters, their husbands, and grown children—all gathered in the small confines of his home. Deep conversations punctuated by furrowed brows ignored the insistent chime of the grandfather clock striking twelve, the familiar sound delivering an ominous tone this December 31, 1939. None of the usual good-humoured embarrassing retells of the retreating year, no lifting and clinking of glasses with spirited cheers of "HURRAY 1940" to toast this new, fresh-faced decade.

The van Cleef twins, Eddy and Jochem, were long since been put to bed. Mirjam, worn out from the day's busyness, had called the evening to a close early. "I'm too exhausted. Midnight is impossible," her hand stifled a yawn, "you know the twins will wake me up like roosters at the dawn."

With a kiss and embrace for her sisters and a nod in the direction of the men, she announced a weary *Gelukkig Neiuwjaar* three hours before its time, and retired down a narrow hall to the flowery wall-papered bedroom at the back of the old brick house on the Afrikanerplein.

Adorable eight-month-old carbon-copy boys lay sleeping side by side in the ornate wooden cradle, its history shared amongst parents, siblings, and sisters. In-laid with a delicate bird and flower motif, the heirloom hand-carved oak bed, worn smooth by a myriad of mothers rocking their babies, had now passed on to her, she being the youngest to start a family.

Trouble was brewing in a disturbed world, but Mirjam, too immersed in motherhood, didn't care to notice. She and Joel had married later in life. Being five years older than her husband, birthing twins at thirty-five was an unexpected miracle, not to mention a superb catch up.

Back up the hall, the men's voices grew heated. "Westerbork is overflowing with German Jews. Thousands fled here and crossed illegally!"—multiple index fingers jabbing the table as if pinpointing the exact location of the alleged crossings.

"Virtually all the Jews in Germany are gone."

"This is true. None are left, their lives strangled by the *Großdeutscher Reichstag*."

"They have driven them, their own people, out."

"So what are we to do with them?"

Voices crawling over voices. Interrupting, conjecturing.

Joel van Cleef owned a small, well-respected leather repair business in the Markenplein square. Re-heeling shoes and work-boots, mending belts, reattaching straps on bags, even repairing heavy horse saddlery marked his days. Whatever his customers brought to him, no matter the condition, his expertise and skill made everything new again. He refused to give up on any task.

Patient customers, Jews and non-Jews alike, standing around waiting for Joel to finish, murmured about the racism problems accelerating in Germany. In shocked disbelief and anxious undertones, last November was recounted, the month Nazi extremists and German citizens, in fits of unrestrained violence smashed windows of Jewish businesses, looting as they went, while the police, casual and disinterested, stood, watched, and did nothing. Joel eavesdropped on it all.

"The *Kristalnacht* could happen here, in Amsterdam, to our shops, to us." The young leather worker, shooting a dark glare at his relatives, stood up, pushed his chair out of the way, and crossed to the other side of the kitchen to grab a drink. He had been on edge for over a year. "If the Germans invade Holland, they will unleash on us the same disgust they showed their own people, or worse."

Life for Germany's Jewish population was so impossible they were fleeing by the thousands into neighbouring countries, trying to immigrate to America, or to any country that would take them in.

"The German Jews are not the problem of the Dutch government." Eliazer was vehement. "Yes, the Germans invaded Poland and yes Britain and France declared war on the Nazis, but Holland must remain neutral! We were neutral in the Great War!" Heads nodded in agreement. "If we stick our noses in now and allow these German refugees to enter and stay, nothing but trouble will follow them."

It was well past midnight and past time to be walking home. The subjects under discussion, however, were too urgent to abandon without reaching some level of consensus and conclusion.

"Germany is our greatest trading partner,"—as if that was sufficient cause for exemption from participation—"they depend on our railways, the most advanced and fastest in Europe,"—still another unlikely stopgap. "No. Holland and Belgium will surely negotiate a peace to keep the trade routes open. We are their direct northern line to France."—an ironic comment considering France was already at war.

"Blind fools," Joel muttered, his voice bitter and tired. "What makes you think we aren't next?" He found such political gesturing irritating.

"Next for what?" Nineteen-year-old Marcus, Joel's nephew, butted into the conversation.

"All of it," was his uncle's terse response.

THE SOFT KNOCKING at the van Cleef's front door disturbed Mirjam's nursing routine. Although barely past 8:00 am, her days started well before dawn, the twins waking early; first one, who invariably unsettled the other. They were teething, turning already brief nights into a constant interruption times two. Joel had long since left for his shop. Covering up, she rose and answered the door, with little Eddy balanced expertly on her left hip.

"*Goedemorgen* Elisabeth, come in, come in! *Wil je een kopje thee?*" The two women greeted each other with heartfelt affection and kinship. "Tell me all the news! Not that I couldn't try harder to strain my ears and catch it all myself with you living so close by."

Clothed in familiarity, Mirjam took her cousin's hand

and bolted the front door. Passing through the entrance hall, they entered a narrow living room. Once inside, Elisabeth kissed her younger cousin on both cheeks, then bent down and swooped up baby Jochem, crawling around her feet.

"I do have some news. Growing news, you could say." Elisabeth, relishing Mirjam's puzzled expression, spontaneously let out an uncharacteristically girlish giggle. The older woman twirled the swung toddler up in the air, then, in one deft move, tucked him under her arm, "It's too early to be certain, but ... you won't believe this ... I'm positive I'm having twins!"

At age forty, Elisabeth Wijnschenk-Hakker already mothered four young ones, all under ten. "I've done this enough times to recognize the signs and let me tell you," her hand rubbed the telltale expanse burgeoning under her dress, "all the signs with this one are in duplicate."

"But wait, there's more!" Elisabeth deposited Jochem on the soft pine floor, its cracked and separated tongue-and-groove joinings revealing its age. *What more could there possibly be?* Mirjam was still trying to digest the news she'd just been fed, "You will NEVER guess what my Salomon installed last week." Before Mirjam could open her mouth to venture a guess, Elisabeth blurted, "A new *stofzuiger*! You know, one of those amazing modern ones with all the attachments that hang on the wall. I've been hinting for months!" Her face glowed as if this announcement carried more weight than her earlier one. Babies? Commonplace. But a new *stofzuiger*? Well, THAT was something to celebrate.

Mirjam burst out laughing. Sitting down, she settled Eddy on her knee, rubbing his back, bottom to top, forcing up any leftover burps. "I'm thrilled for you. For your future babies—may they be born safe—and certainly, the arrival of a fancy-shmancy new vacuum cleaner, too!" Mirjam's eyes danced as she laughed again, "Your floor will be cleaner than mine. I'm coming to your house with my crawling children!"

The other twin scooted by. "Here, take Eddy." Mirjam blindly passed the infant to her cousin as she jumped up to grab the dashing crawler. Eyes sparkling with hidden excitement, she pointed to her recently vacated chair. "Please, sit down ... I can add to your news." Now it was Elisabeth's turn to be held in suspense. Mirjam's whole being strained to contain the secret their younger cousin had whispered to her a few months ago. "You're not the only one having twins." She paused and looked around, as if someone might secretly be listening. "So is Helena!"

Over steaming cups of black tea, they chatted about life and love, babies and children, food and family. And their men. They worried about their men. Husbands obsessed with politics, pouring over the news and arguing about a possible war looming on the horizon, its potential evil hovering like a doom-filled thundercloud over the borders of the Netherlands.

The twins, lulled by the soothing rhythm of the gentle rise and fall of voices, fell asleep in the women's arms, one identical bundle of innocence for each. Mirjam and Elisabeth marvelled at the thought of three sets of twins born into the family, within nine months of each other. They talked of them growing up and learning together, becoming friends by choice, sharing all the wonderful times waiting for them in the futures of their lives.

"Have you ever heard of another family with as many sets of twins as ours?" There passed an incredulous glance at the sleeping boys, then at each other.

～

WITHOUT WARNING, sirens shattered the silence of the otherwise still, spring-like morning of May 10, 1940. Dutch people throughout the country were shaken out of their beds by the terrifying sound of aircraft engines filling the sky. Germany had invaded the Netherlands.

Four days later, with the unprepared Dutch army utterly defeated and the 600-year-old city of Rotterdam bombed to the ground, Holland surrendered.

THE LONG NIGHT of August 23, 1940, was unseasonably hot, windless, and humid for a usually breezy, moderate northern climate. Elisabeth, her older sisters Mietje and Esther assisting, and Salomon, her husband, at her side, safely delivered her twin boys, Abraham and Tobias. Elisabeth, strong and determined, laboured through her delivery virtually silent. Four other sleeping children did not need their dreams disturbed by the hard arrival of life unfolding down the hall.

With five girls in the family, Elisabeth had herself stood as midwife for the others, and could have managed with only Salomon, but her sisters were adamant. "Miss the birth of another set of twins? Never!" Mietje, bossy, matronly, and the eldest, sloshed birth-stained towels in an old enamel washbasin arranged on the bedside table newly placed near the only open window. Pushing the lace curtains aside, she longed for a light breeze to freshen the oppressive air.

"Why, it was worth staying up late, sweating all these hours, to take care of you and be the first witness to another miracle." Mietje wiped her hands, then hung the towels on the wooden rack under the window to dry, a near impossibility with the humidity clinging to everything and everyone.

"And now she has two more handsome boys to add to her existing collection of three!" A proud, deep voice boomed across the room. Salomon Hakker loved his wife, loved his family, and absolutely adored his only daughter, Helena.

He was a reliable hard worker, and lucky to have a stable job at his father's fruit and vegetable market. Many a day he arrived home with unsaleable store produce past its prime. "Perfect for soup," Elisabeth would announce, thankful for the addition to their pantry. They managed, even with such an extensive family, increased by two this night. Life was full; their days content.

"Our Helena will have a glorious time mothering them." Nine years and three miscarriages separated Helena from these newcomers, Tobias and Abraham. She had been hoping for a baby sister, or sisters! But tiny brothers to boss around would be just as much fun. Powerless and defenceless against her supreme might, she imagined dressing them up in girl-clothes, and wheeling them proudly about the neighbourhood.

"Shhh. Elisabeth needs to rest, and the babies too." Thoughtful, always gentle Esther swaddled the newborns and placed them on her sister's chest, one for each side. "Don't worry about a thing, *mijn lieve zus*. You have four sisters. They are all the extra hands you need." Her loving touch smoothed out a few creases disturbing the fresh bed sheets. "*Moeder* would be proud of you." A moment of sadness lingered between sisters at the mention of their mother. She had died young. What deep satisfaction and happiness it would have given her to know she had, in total, twenty-seven healthy grandchildren and great-grandchildren.

Mietje brightened up, "At least you didn't have triplets like our great-great-grandmother, Schoontje Wijnschenk! Can you even imagine what that would have been like, a hundred years ago?" An involuntary chorus of exhausted groans at the mere thought of such a marathon escaped from the family cloistered in the tiny hothouse of a bedroom. Esther, swaying back and forth, hummed softly and nuzzled a fragrant, fuzzy baby head.

Babies are a blessing,
whether one or three,
and bring good luck
to every family.

"THIS IS UTTER NONSENSE, absolute garbage! They can't possibly be serious. *Godverdomme!*" Glaring at the document in his hand, dated September 20, 1940, Mozes Zwaaf, red-faced and eyes glaring, paced the well-worn floor of his small fruit store and butcher shop on the Blasiusstraat. "They expect me to report all my business assets to the German civil administration here in Amsterdam? The bloody SS will have their greedy hands on me!" The paper ripped as he flung it across the floor.

This new decree came on the heels of an announcement that all Jewish civil servants were to be let go, and all Jewish newspapers forced to shut down. "What's next?" Mozes was still pacing and muttering. "They want our bank accounts, our personal assets? What, they will need lace curtains, children's toys and china dishes too!?"

Jacob, his second son and manager of the store, paused from inventorying a new arrival of fresh produce and appeared from around the back corner, worried at the sudden commotion. Mozes angrily gestured towards the paper on the floor. Retrieving the torn document, Jacob glanced at it before handing it back to his father. Together they scoured over the announcement, the same one destined to be delivered to every Jewish business in the city.

"I can't tell Helena, not yet," a resigned decision uttered only to himself. "The twins are due in a month."

ELISABETH BOUNCED HER ONE-MONTH-OLD BABIES, asleep in their pram, over the rough cobblestones to Mirjam's house, a mere two minutes journey. Helena's twins had been born—almost too soon. Although Helena was one of twelve brothers and sisters, only her sister, Sientje, lived close enough to be available and on call when Helena's time came, and come it did, three weeks early.

"Oh, they are so tiny!" Mirjam and Elisabeth bent with adulation over the newborn Zwaaf twins, Eva and Mozes. "And a girl! You have girl. You named her after your mother!" The women were beside themselves with maternal glee. "She's absolutely adorable. Look at all that hair!"

Two identically faced cherubic boys, Mirjam's eighteen-month-old twins, toddled past to have a sneak peek at these new cousins. Pudgy hands pulled at the lemon-yellow and sky-blue crocheted blankets, but with these new interlopers offering little in terms of entertainment, they wandered off to play with the matching set of little wooden cars their Opa van Cleef had hand-carved for them.

"I can't imagine my babies ever getting so big," Elisabeth, almost envious, fought off an urge to compare her scrunchy-faced, helpless month-old twins to Mirjam's round-faced, bow-legged toddlers.

"Oh stop Elisabeth. Before long your Toby and Abraham will celebrate their birthday and be put on display in the grand family Twin Line, and you'll be signing them up for school. OH! I just realized! They'll be in the same grade as Helena's children. Think of all the fun they'll have together." Mirjam rambled on while helping change little Eva, a miniature doll wrapped in a miniature triangle of white flannel nappy cloth.

The inevitable female inquisition bubbled up. "How are you managing? What does the doctor say? Are the babies healthy? Are you getting any sleep at all? How is the pain when you walk? We know what it's like to be feeding two! How *are* you?"

The youngest of the three new mothers in the room offered a weary but satisfied smile. "It's all fine, really. My sister, Sientje, is a great help." Helena paused, blushing slightly, "Nursing is a bit of a shock. It's oppressive. There's no getting away from it ... and so painful." Understanding looks and nods acknowledged such personal comments. "I'm nothing but a glorified milk cow on two legs." Sudden laughter filled the room at Helena's unexpected remark. "Yes, I am tired all the time. But really, we're managing."

"You're so young, Helena, with your entire life ahead of you, and the lives of these babies to enrich it." Elisabeth offered encouragement, although she herself was feeling her age, the struggle to recover from birthing twins taking its toll. "You'll be back to yourself before you know it and doing all the things you did before."

Sientje, the self-proclaimed nurse on-call, entered

with a delectable assortment of cookies on an heirloom silver tray, her own shy little four-year-old daughter, another Eva namesake, trailing along behind.

1941 - *UNBELIEVABLE*

ALL JEWS ARE REQUIRED TO REGISTER THEMSELVES WITH THE LOCAL AUTHORITIES ALONG WITH ALL MEMBERS OF THEIR IMMEDIATE FAMILY.

ALL INDIVIDUALS WITH AT LEAST ONE JEWISH GRANDPARENT ARE REQUIRED TO REGISTER THEMSELVES WITH THE LOCAL AUTHORITIES.

ALL MIXED MARRIAGES WITH JEWS ARE REQUIRED TO REGISTER THEMSELVES AND THEIR SPOUSES WITH THE LOCAL AUTHORITIES ALONG WITH THE RELIGIOUS AFFILIATION AND NAMES OF ALL GRANDPARENTS.

SALOMON AND ELISABETH HAKKER stood and stared with shocked disbelief at *Het Joodse Weekblad*, the Jewish Weekly, copies of which were plastered conspicuously around Amsterdam, this one covering the front window of the Zwaaf Family butcher shop.

Another New Year, another cloying layer of oppression. Bit by bit, word by word, the freedom enjoyed by legal Dutch citizens for centuries was being stripped away from those whom the Germans deemed Jewish. Husband and wife shared a silent look, one overlaid with mutual dread and a deep, instinctive fear. Undercurrents of conversations hummed around them; an ebb of emotion rising on subdued thought now finding voice and commonality.

Everyone must register names and addresses

- *What for?*
- *Why only us?*
- *I'm not Jewish anymore; I converted to Catholicism.*
- *I never knew my grandparents; they died before I was born.*
- *We are not religious. We know nothing about Judaism.*
- *I married an Italian. Why should I register?*
- *How can the Dutch government allow this to happen?*
- *We have rights as Dutch citizens!*
- *It's started, you know. They will hunt us all down.*
- *Why do they need the names of babies and children?*
- *No one is safe, not even in their own home.*
- *What have we done to make them hate us so much?*

∼

"MAMA WE GO PARK?" Three-year-old Eddy tugged at his mother's ankle-length black linen skirt. "Papa come?" Joel van Cleef set his woodworking aside and squatted, face-level with the little twin. "No, *mannetje*, we cannot go to the park today."

Eddy's lower lip began to tremble, his hazel, long-lashed eyes brimming with tears. For all their little lives, almost every day, the twins played at the *Wibautpark*, a quick three-minute walk from their home, often with their next-door twin cousins, Eva and Mozes Zwaaf. "Morrow?" Jochem's turn to ask. "We go morrow? Mozie Evie too?"

Mirjam's face fell as her children's father took both boys into his arms and buried his tears in their little mop-haired heads. He inhaled the fragrance of them; so clean, so fresh, so universally innocent.

For them, life had disintegrated into an unrelenting choking of normalcy: no more parks, no more beaches, no more Sunday walks, no more ice cream or oranges ... no more sunshine on their side of the street.

1942 - *UNDENIABLE*

"Helena! Come, please. Hurry, hide this!" Jacob Zwaaf pressed a small package wrapped in plain butcher paper with *lever* in block letters written across the front into her hands. "You must go, now, to the house of your relative, Betje Vittali. Give this to her husband, Giovanni." Helena felt the package in her hands, fingers blindly fumbling to locate its contents. "It's our wedding rings, your mother's gold ten-guilder-piece necklace, and the diamond earrings from your grandmother."

Helena stared down at the humble-looking parcel thrust into her possession. "Tell him to keep it safe—any way he can. Giovanni is a good man. He will understand what we are asking him to do." Helena threw a worried look up at her husband. "Don't fret. I'll stay with the twins until you're back."

Eva and Mozes deftly crawled out from under the ornate carved legs of the kitchen table made by their father, scooted across the hard floor to the front room and back again, endlessly trailing after the family's long-haired, long-suffering ginger cat. Born as tiny preemies, they were now a healthy, robust, inseparable duo; Mozes crowned with a shock of flaming red, poker-straight hair and Eva, a perfect little princess with enviable jet-black curls.

"Hurry! Please hurry and leave." Tense and determined, his body betraying a visceral sense of urgency, Jacob was almost shoving his young wife out the door. "Rumours are growing. We are soon to be branded, identifiable in public in front of everyone, forced to wear a yellow star."

Helena said nothing. He was frightening her, the wild look in his eyes filling her with dread. In her mind she could see the six-pointed-star, an instantly recognizable symbol of Judaism eliciting many mixed emotions: pride, heroism, indifference, fear, prejudice, aversion, shame. Yellow. On the one hand, the colour of sunshine, joy, and childlike energy, and on the other, danger, jealousy, and betrayal.

Jacob carried on, "Can you believe it? We will stand out in any crowd. Targets of abuse with no place to hide." As he spat out his bits of unsettling news, Jacob's face hardened, the recent years of increased frustration and continual helplessness etching a map of worry across his forehead. "And our own young women forced to make them in the sewing factories."

Thirty-year-old Helena hurried into her warm, blue woollen overcoat, draping a knitted scarf over her head and around her neck before tucking the ends securely down the coat front. Though early spring warmed the soil and tulip tips poked red out of the welcoming earth, a definite chill wrapped the air. The Amstel River, on more than one occasion during the past few weeks, greeted the morning with a shimmering veil of paper-thin ice.

The walk to the Vittali home on the Amsteldijk was only fifteen minutes away—a safe route, along main streets. Once across the *Nieuwe Amstelbrug* bridging the Amstel River, she would be there. Helena tucked her small brown package in an inside pocket—secure, hidden, secret. She started for the door, hugged her arms across her chest as if protecting not only her family's jewellery but her very self, and left.

THE SUDDEN KNOCKING on the door came hard and insistent—but it was not the welcoming knock of a trusted neighbour or close relative. "This is the family of the Jew, Joel van Cleef?" The German SS soldier looming before her appeared young, almost a teenager, the confidence of a mature, hardened Nazi not yet present in his nervous demeanour.

"Yes," Mirjam's voice trembled, swallowing the terror rising in her throat. She wondered if his mother knew where he was and what he was doing. Her eyes sought his face for any signs of empathy. She wondered if he knew what he was doing.

"You and your immediate family are required to report to the Amsterdam train station on July 1, 1942." The officer read the names of Joel, Mirjam, and their two sons, Eddy and Jochem, in a disinterested voice devoid of human emotion. "These are the members of your family?"

"Yes," Mirjam answered singularly again.

"Give this document to your husband." A sharp *Hiel Hitler* salute sent Mirjam reeling backwards into the doorway. The boy soldier whirled around, turned his back on her, and was gone.

"Well, if there's one thing we Jewish people have mastered, it is following and obeying rules." Joel's voice cut a sarcastic and bitter tone as he shredded the document handed him by his wife.

All Dutch Jews were encouraged, and expected, to heed all requests of the new, German-formed Jewish Council. This meant registering family members, reporting for "evacuation" when called, not complaining or arguing, and generally not causing trouble, thus avoiding making matters worse for everyone —supposedly.

~

"WHAT, we are sheep? Expected to follow any order like dumb animals?" The crowd's confusion and anger mounted. "Where are we going? When, and what for?" A long line of people was forming outside the Jewish Council address, everyone gesticulating the same questions. Eight-hundred men, women and children all newly called to report for systematic removal to labour camps.

Joel was not convinced of this urgent plea for obedient workers. "What do you do with children and babies at a labour camp?" His eye fell on the many frail and elderly among the crowd, not a one of them with enough stamina or muscle to lift a shovel or drag rocks.

Around him, whisperings of those gone into hiding, names he did not want to overhear. *Trying to hide is far more dangerous than deportation*, that much he believed, *but how can one hide an entire family? How could you separate twins?* Both were unknown options, but at least there should be more safety in numbers, however implausible the purpose.

On July 1, 1942, Joel and Mirjam van Cleef, dutifully, and as directed, placed all their possessions and money in the care of the German established LIRO Bank, paid for two full-price adult and two half-price children's one-way tickets to not even God knows where, and boarded the train.

"HELENA, have you gotten any letters from Mirjam?" Two months had passed and Elisabeth, despite having written almost every week, never received so much as a postcard response from her cousin. Elisabeth suffered a deep emptiness at Mirjam's leaving. It was a rare day that had not seen the two of them checking in, easing the care of children, sharing the joy of watching their twins play and grow together.

"Nothing." Helena's tone, dry and lifeless as she started into a tirade, "Not a single word from any of our family since they left. And we've now gotten our own deportation letter. Can you believe we have to buy our own fare, for the twins and ourselves? Idiots! They force us to go, but make us pay full price! My Jacob believes because we are young and strong, as long as we work hard and do as we are told, no matter how bad it is, we can wait out the war in the labour camp."

Helena's face spat out disgust and disbelief.

Elisabeth's had aged, more so since her other young cousin, Lea, and infant son, Robert, had disappeared. They had not been seen for many weeks. Gossip and rumours circulated that they ignored their deportation letter and escaped into hiding with the help of the Dutch Resistance. But that was only a hunch. No one dared talk about such things openly. How do you disappear in a country as small, flat, and densely populated as Holland?

And the trains—each week, every Tuesday, the trains —each one filled to overflowing with obedient Dutch Jewish citizens from every walk of life, every age. Hundreds upon hundreds upon hundreds. How many "workers" did this totalitarian German regime require for its slave labour force? Where was the food to feed them all going to come from and the rooms to house them all? Supplies were already hitting dangerous lows in the cities, and rationing was strictly enforced.

The unsettling sentiment echoing throughout the community for months raised its voice again. What in heaven's name would the Germans do with grandparents and babies? This didn't seem like a necessary part of war. This was something else.

Elisabeth received no replies to any of her letters from Helena, either.

1943 - *INEVITABLE*

The banging on the door was so brutal, the twins woke up screaming from such a violent and abrupt intrusion into their dreams. Before Salomon Hakker could even reach for the doorknob, five SS Nazi soldiers broke into his house, eyes blazing with a loathsome hate for having to enter the despicable home of an *aschmutziges Jüdisches Schwein*.

"You have three sons, yes?" barked an unidentified voice.

Salomon stared back hard, his body blocking the men from entering any further. "You need to ask? Are you so stupid? You and your spies already know who lives in my house." A split second, and a blunt pistol smashes Salomon across the side of his head, sending the 6' 2" burly man careening to the floor, hands sheltering his face, blood pouring out of his nose.

"Enough! Stop it! Leave him alone!" Twenty-one-year-old Mozes Hakker helps his father to his feet, then turns to face the Nazis standing in his home, the place of his birth, his childhood; the sacred centre of all the memories of a life surrounded by love, kindness, and self-sacrifice.

"What do you want with me and my brothers?" Harry, sixteen, and Jacques, nineteen, appear from the shelter of the kitchen and stand, hesitant, beside their brother and father.

The same Nazi soldier that assaulted Salomon points his pistol at the young men. "You three are to come with us. You are being sent to a work camp for labour detail immediately. If you resist, you will be shot."

Out of sight in a back bedroom, Elisabeth and Helena, hiding, anxiously hush the twins as fractured sounds and scattered voices drift jagged down the hallway.

Helena, in grade five at school, was already witness to the diminishing attendance of her schoolmates. Each week, fewer were in class. Some, dutifully reporting for deportation with their families, others, refusing to follow orders, taken by aggression, and still others, gone without a trace.

"They are here for us, all of us," Helena said, her

voice evidencing a sombre knowledge of things far beyond that of any normal eleven-year-old. Her present life had become anything but normal. Innocence and childhood halted, arrested and dragged away, long before their time.

A few moments later, a door slams. In its place, deathly silence.

BETJE VITTALI, her cousin Elisabeth, and sister-in-law Mina, sat, nerves on edge, in Mina's front room, its heavy curtains drawn shut, casting the room into a gloomy darkness. Long thin fingers of sunlight poked through gaps in the fabric, filaments of invisible dust discovered and made visible only by the penetrating, searching light.

Two coats displaying stitched yellow stars lay folded, displayed on the single chair in the entry. Another, similarly branded, hung on the ornate oak coat rack standing guard in the corner.

Conversations, like their lives, fragmented, unfocussed, and occasionally, almost incoherent. One topic usurped another, dropped midway in the face of yet another. Each one urgent, each one desperate to be pulled to the surface, the unburdening of them shared in hushed mutual confidence, softened, wept over, and fought against.

Eight long months had passed since the seizure of Elisabeth's boys, yet not one word from any of them. No news of Mirjam, her husband and children, or of Helena and hers. Or, if they dared admit it, of anyone else.

In disquieted tones, the women discussed a list of family no longer in Amsterdam and elsewhere. Had they heard? Their oldest cousin in Groningen, Abraham

Goudsmit — deported one month after his ninetieth birthday. *Verschrikkelijk!* How is it possible that any human being, with any semblance of conscience, could remove a ninety-year-old man from his home and send him to a slave-labour work camp in a far-off foreign country? *Goeie hemel.*

The three of them sat motionless, resigned to what their world had become, what it was for others, and what it could still be for them. The incessant ticking of the antique oak grandfather clock resonated in the silent spaces between conversations.

They latched onto a few bleak discussions of family hope. Lea and Robbie de Vries, safe in hiding. Jacob Hijman, along with his young family and wife, reported to have somehow escaped off a train and fled to Switzerland. Sheltered behind the heavy, dark drapes, they shared hushed reports of babies and children smuggled out of the city in bags and boxes, and into the care of strangers.

These hopes thinned when compared to the arrest and deportation of siblings with families, aunts and uncles, grown cousins, neighbours and friends. They whispered confessions of the dangerous secrets they housed, trading them with each other, needing some relief from the weight of carrying such burdens.

The only other bright spots in the room, save the finger-lights, were the twins. No longer helpless, toothless infants, the boys, Tobias and Abraham, soon to be three years old, sat, chubby-faced and big-eyed, eating as many cookies as Tante Mina was allowed to give them.

~

"SALOMON!" Elisabeth strained her head above the crowd in the Amsterdam open square. They had separated by accident, he with Helena, and she with the twins. "SALOMON!!" A sickening fear rose in her throat as she squeezed the boys' hands harder, pulling them sharply closer. Elisabeth pushed through the usual display of Friday afternoon gatherers: housewives selecting their allotment of rationed fish, bread, and vegetables, bystanders observing, the Dutch police mingling and watching.

Out of nowhere, a piercing whistle shatters the air. In an instant, swarms of German SS flank the market, yelling expletives at the top of their lungs and barking orders that no one understands. Swastika symbols, notorious black emblems emblazoned on red armbands, mark the SS from their Dutch equivalents. Pistol shots fire into the air and the entire square explodes into panic.

Razzia! Within minutes, every chest bearing a star is brutally shoved and singled out. Terrified people are thrown to their knees: old, weathered men, elderly women hugging meagre baskets of food, mothers struggling with screaming children and babies, young people lifting brave, defiant faces.

Panicked and disoriented, Elisabeth's heart pounds in her ears as she kneels on the ancient cobblestones, loose shards of tiny stone digging into her flesh. Instinctively, she shoves the twins under her coat for protection, almost smothering them.

A firm hand grabs her by the shoulder, forcing her to catch her breath, an involuntary, sharp response. Elisabeth whirls her head around. Oh, thank God! It's Salomon, holding Helena close to his side, providing what little level of safety he can. In a husky voice, thick with emotion, he whispers in his wife's ear, "We stay together. We will always stay together."

The once placid market is a terrifying scene of hapless humanity, supreme power versus absolute powerlessness. At gunpoint, people are piled into military trucks and driven off; random arms, as if disjointed from bodies, dangling out the sides for lack of space.

As quickly as it began, the razzia ends. As the telltale fumes of diesel linger in the air, the market resumes its pace, empty spaces of the missing filled by the casualness of the newly arrived, unaware and oblivious. What can they do? This is life now.

Whatever traces remain of those taken are washed away like grains of sand pounded to nothing under the force of a relentless, unstoppable wave.

AFTERMATH

A careful review of my family's genealogical records, compared with historical records and dates, revealed that the van Cleef family would have been among the very first group of Jews deported from Holland, and that Mirjam and her three-year-old twins were killed immediately upon arrival at the newly completed Auschwitz *Endlösung der Judenfrage* complex in German-occupied southern Poland.

After members of the Hakker family were rounded up and arrested, they would have been forced into a truck or put on a train, and taken to Westerbork. From there, the family would have been held until transportation to Auschwitz, where again, immediately upon arrival, the entire remaining family was gassed. The three older boys, Mozes, Jacques and Harry, had already been transported and killed eight months earlier.

the van Cleef family

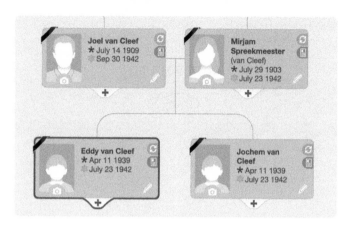

the Zwaaf family

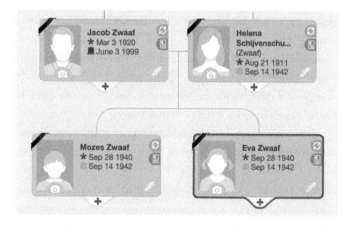

All Jewish people in German-occupied countries were forced to surrender the value of their bank accounts, valuables, insurance policies, stocks, bonds, jewellery, artwork, household goods, literally any and everything of value. It is estimated that the Nazi regime stole, in today's value, over $10 billion from Europe's Jews—insidiously stockpiling effortless financial fuel for their war machine.

The following items were confiscated from Salomon and Elisabeth Hakker's home, and deposited to the LIRO bank for "safekeeping". Note the contents of the corridor.

BEDROOM
    lace curtain (2)
    drape (3)
    hanging lamp
    wall mirror
    wooden bedstead with bedding
    cot with bedding (2)
    alarm clock
    bookcase with children's books
    table
    chair (2)
    wall cupboard with ladies' clothing
    floorcloth and runner

Room
    cooker

BEDROOM
    hanging lamp
    bedside table
    chair (2)
    iron bedstead with bedding
    linen cupboard with linen
    floorcloth and runner

          • • •

BEDROOM

    lace curtain (2)

    wall plate (2)

    iron bedstead with bedding

    wall cupboard with clothing, knick-knacks

    floorcloth and runner

CORRIDOR

    hanging lamp

    coat hooks

    wall cupboard with vacuum cleaner (Protos)

KITCHEN

    lace curtain (2)

    lamp

    wall mirror

    coffee grinder

    rack with enamelware

    gas stove with 2 burners

    table

    chair

    display cabinet

    ceramics

    cooking utensils

∾

The Hakker Family

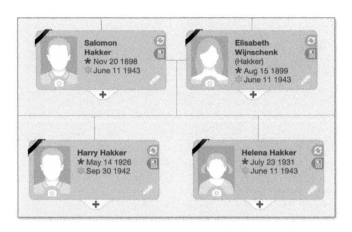

Salomon Hakker
★ Nov 20 1898
☙ June 11 1943

Elisabeth Wijnschenk (Hakker)
★ Aug 15 1899
☙ June 11 1943

Harry Hakker
★ May 14 1926
☙ Sep 30 1942

Helena Hakker
★ July 23 1931
☙ June 11 1943

Tobias Hakker
★ Aug 23 1940
☙ June 11 1943

Abraham Hakker
★ Aug 23 1940
☙ June 11 1943

Mozes Hakker
★ Feb 7 1921
☙ Sep 30 1942

Jacques Hakker
★ July 3 1923
☙ Sep 30 1942

2017 - KINGSTON

MYSTERY

*S*urely a handful of pictures exists somewhere. Old photographs locked up in archives or identified by some obscure source must have found their way on to the internet by now. One more time … search all the names … again.

January 2, 2017

https://coenraadrood.org/en

I'm flabbergasted. My mother's list, in its entirety and more, is on the IN MEMORIAM section of a website I've never seen, recounting the stories of people I do not know.

A new Google search of my great-grandfather, Levie Hijman, had brought up a startling and utterly unexpected link. Why would my family's names be included on this website? Who put them there?

I scour every page, every picture, every video on the

site hoping for clues, but there are no discernible connections. It is a total mystery. A new journey begins.

January 2, 2017
-----Oorspronkelijk bericht-----

contacthco@historischcentrumoverijssel.nl
Verzonden: maandag 2 januari 2017 17:16
Aan: contacthco
Onderwerp: Formulierinzending
van: Contactformulier

--Contactformulier--

Aanhef: mevrouw
Naam: Stella ter Hart
Plaats: CANADA
Onderwerp: Persinformatie
Vraag of opmerking:

Hello from Canada. While researching my family ancestry, I was shocked to discover the names of many of my family members who died in concentration camps listed in the 'In Memoriam' section of the Coenraad Rood website:
https://www.coenraadrood.org/en/info

My great grandfather was Levie Hijman. Please, do you know any more about why my family is in the *In Memoriam* section of this website? Coen must have known them! How can I find out more information? Thank you so much for any help.

Stella ter Hart

January 13, 2017

Dag mevr. ter Hart,

Ik heb uw vraag uitgezet bij 2 mensen, buiten onze organisatie, die de basis hebben gelegd voor de realisatie van de website over Coenraad Rood in de hoop dat zij u kunnen helpen bij uw zoektocht naar nadere informatie over uw familieleden. Zo gauw als ik iets hoor, laat ik u dit weten.

Met vriendelijke groet, Marieke

Marieke Steegmans
Publieksactiviteiten,
Vrijwilligers

Historisch Centrum Overijssel
Van Wevelinkhovenstraat, Zwolle
Post & parkeren: Eikenstraat 20, 8021 WX Zwolle

January 23, 2017

> *Van: Stella*
> *Verzonden: maandag 23 januari 2017 01:53*
> *Aan: gjw@kliksafe.nl*
> *Onderwerp:*
> *Formulierinzending van: Contactformulier*

Lieve Gertjan,

My apologies that my Dutch is not good enough to write

in, so I must use English. I am able to read Dutch quite well, but have little experience in writing in Dutch. Marieke has been so kind as to give me your contact name and email.

I am the great grand daughter of Levie Hijman. My Oma, Elisabeth Vittali (Hijman), was the only surviving child of Levie, who, along with all of his adult children, their children and grandchildren, were all killed in the camps. I do not have a complete history, but have all of their names. My Oma was married to an Italian, so was not deported.

My question is this: why is my great grandfather, and many, many of his family, listed in the IN MEMORIAM section of this page of the website: https://www.coenraadrood.org/en/info. Is it possible that Meneer Rood knew my family? And if so, are there any stories about them? They are not mentioned specifically in the videos.

I would be ever grateful for any insight. Thank you!

Stella ter Hart

January 31, 2017

Re: Formulierinzending
van: Contactformulier

Good evening Stella,

Last week I received your mail. I have talked with Coen

Rood very often, by skype. But in all the hours we did meet, he didn't tell me about Levie Hijman.

In 2012 I published a book about the jewish camps in Staphorst en Rouveen. On the last pages of the book I made a list of names of the men that did live in those camps. On page 120 stands Hakker Heijman, 01-05-1890 Amsterdam. But that name is not exactly the same as your Hijman. So I do not know or I have made a little mistake by writing the name. Or maybe it is another family. This is all the information I have. I am afraid I cannot help you for more information.

Kind regards,
Gert-Jan Westhoff

January 31, 2017

Dag Stella ter Hart,

Nog aanvullend op uw mail aan ons, kan ik u berichten dat de namen op de website Coenraad Rood op verzoek van **Samuel Wennek** indertijd zijn toegevoegd. Mogelijk dat hij u verder kan helpen.

Met vriendelijke groet, Marieke

Marieke Steegmans
Publieksactiviteiten, Vrijwilligers
Historisch Centrum Overijssel
Van Wevelinkhovenstraat, Zwolle

April 4, 2017

Re:
website Coenraad Rood and familie Hijman

Good morning Samuel,

I am the daughter of Sophia Maria ter Hart (geboren Vittali). My mother passed away last year and recently I was with my father cleaning out her papers.

I discovered some email correspondence between you and her, and our relatives. Your name also was a surprise to see in the email correspondence below with Marieke Steegmans from the Historisch Centrum Overijssel which you can read.

My mother never talked to her children about the events of the war very much, and we were never allowed to bring it up or discuss it at all. I know some, but now that she is gone, have been digging to find as much as I can.

I am sorry that I cannot write to you in Dutch.

I would be very honoured to correspond with you as we are family connected by such a tragic past.

I hope you are well,
Stella ter Hart

～

April 4, 2017

Re: website Coenraad Rood and familie Hijman

Good day Stella,

Most appreciative to receive your email, its always good
to hear from family no matter how distant they may be.

Indeed we are family my grandmother and your
grandmother were daughters of the late Levi Hijman who
together with many members of our family was murdered
in those terrible and sad circumstances during the period
1942/45. The names that appear on the coenrood.org site
were a condition of our sponsorship of this educative
Internet site.

Incredible. Exhilarating.

Almost unbelievable.

After over 300 days of painstaking research, the only result of which was the tragic uncovering of family members long gone, I finally discover a family member very much alive.

HIDDEN

*T*he day Levie and Tilly Wennek received their orders to report to the *Hollandsche Schouwburg*, they had little choice but to obey. The razzias had become more and more frequent, and more and more violent. Any pretences of civility on the part of the Germans occupying Holland had long since vanished away.

Tilly's parents, Henri and Engeltje Kattenburg, received the same letter, with instructions to report to the same place at the same time as their eldest daughter, Mathilda, her husband, Levie, and their only son, four-year-old Samuel.

Previously enjoyed as a luxurious and renowned performing arts theatre, the *Schouwburg* was now gutted and converted into an incarceration area for Jews awaiting transportation to Westerbork or Vught before deportation to the concentration camps.

When rumours of the intimidation and aggressive actions against German Jews reached Holland, Henri Kattenburg sent his son, Andries, to New York in 1940. As his two daughters Mathilda and Rachel were both married with small children, it was impossible to arrange immigration to America for so many. Though a wealthy and influential businessman and joint-owner of the Kattenburg Textile Factory, even he could only pull so many strings.

The one individual Henri trusted above everyone else was Giovanni Vittali, his only non-Jewish relative, the husband of his wife's closest sister. In secret, with instructions to keep it safe until after the war, he gave Giovanni ƒ100,000 Dutch guilders in cash, funds hidden and not reported to the Germans. Funds that would be no use to Henri wherever he was going but would undoubtedly have been of significant use to the Nazis.

If Henri had been caught with the funds, if Giovanni was caught with the funds ...

over my dead body

∼

Tuesday, July 13, 1943

"Daddy, are we going on a holiday? Can we go to the beach now? It's so hot!" Four-year-old Samuel gripped a handful of carrot-red hair, steadying himself as he perched on his father's shoulders, his own blonde head jutting above the crowd. "Why are so many people here? Everyone has a suitcase. Where is everybody going? Are they all going on a vacation? Look! I see Oma and Opa!"

The Kattenburg's little grandson, all smiles and chatter and dimples, threw both arms up over his head to greet his grandparents, who were struggling their way through the crush of strangers towards him. A wall of people surrounded them, all dragging bags and boxes, suitcases and purses. Children, pointing curiously, posed an endless barrage of questions to grim-faced and tight-lipped adults.

Some men, dressed in funny clothes and talking loudly in words Samuel did not understand, were carrying sticks and rifles, and waving them in the air at people. The men kept yelling and made everyone stand in a line holding a special paper. Samuel had to stand on the ground now, behind his grandparents, and between his father and mother. He wished his father would pick him up again. All he could see were knees.

When it was their turn for the angry-faced men to take away their paper, one of them pointed off to the side to a strange, big, dirty truck that was being loaded with all the Opas and Omas. With a rude shove, he pushed Samuel's grandparents towards the truck, and Samuel, puzzled, watched them climb in. They turned to him, gave a gigantic smile, and waved continuously. Samuel tried waving back as long as he could, but his arm became too tired. Oma blew him kisses until he could not see her anymore.

Something inside Samuel knew they were not going on a holiday. He didn't like the angry men in strange clothes with spiders on their arms. They took him and his parents to a police station where they had to wait in another line for a very long time. "Mama, I don't want to stand," whispered Samuel, a plaintive face looking up at Mathilda, "My legs are tired of holding me up."

"Shhhhh, *schatje*," she said, bending over to tousle his curly head. "Be a good boy for just a teeny bit longer."

Another angry-faced man wearing the same funny clothes as the other angry-faced men leaned over his desk and glared at Samuel, who was barely tall enough to be seen over the top of it. Grabbing the special paper his father was still holding, the angry man hit it so hard with a stamp that Samuel jumped, then laid their paper on a pile with all the other special papers. Samuel and his parents were pushed into a different line again, forced outside into the dark, and herded down the street. They did not stop until they reached a big, white building. Everyone went inside.

Samuel wondered what was for supper. Not only were his legs tired of holding him up, his tummy was tired of being empty. He missed his Oma. She always made him delicious things for supper.

THE YOUNG WOMAN, coyly dressed in a blue flared woollen skirt, close-fitting white top embroidered with blue and white flowers, and matching blue scarf, pulled Tilly aside and spoke in a guarded, earnest voice. "I see on the records that you have only one child, a sweet, Dutch-looking blonde boy." The two shared a cautious glance. Tilly came in closer, lowering her head, and came alongside the young woman, their shoulders touching. "Listen carefully. We can take him, and hide him in good, safe Dutch homes. He will not be discovered, I promise." Tilly said nothing, but she was listening. Eyes wide, the girl carried on. "What do the Nazis want with children at these supposed work camps? Let us save him. We do it every day, right underneath the noses of these arrogant Germans."

A defiant look crossed her face. Nellie worked at the Dutch daycare and nursery located inside the Teacher's Training College, directly across the street from where Tilly and Levie were being held. Samuel, along with the other children separated from their parents, was housed at the daycare. The German guards policing the theatre had no patience for crying babies and whining toddlers.

"But you have to decide, and fast. We cannot wait, and if you cannot decide, I have to choose another child." Mathilda turned away, the shadows under her eyes suddenly darker. Her heart pounded, despair and panic rising in her chest. If Samuel was not near her, how could she protect him? He was so little, so confused. Would he feel abandoned, thrown away? Would he survive? On the other hand, were any of us trapped here going to survive.

Once gone, it would be as if he was never hers. Samuel would become a secret, one never to admit, not even under torture. Precipitantly, she was being asked to thrust her only son away into an unknown future, out of her hands and out of her sight. What kind of mother does such a thing?

"If you agree, I will smuggle him away tomorrow morning as we leave the nursery."

Small groups of children, all various ages and sizes, were often seen leaving the daycare. Led by their caregivers, they were allowed to take a daily walk. Nellie straightened up, tossed back her attractive blonde head and let out a soft laugh. "I flirt with whatever Nazi is on duty, take ten children out for a few hours and come back with nine. They don't even notice if one is missing. They only notice my legs."

The next morning, Samuel is slipped into the small crowd of youngsters heading outside, and disappears into the underground world of the Dutch Resistance. He would never see his parents or grandparents again.

∾

AFTER HIS ESCAPE, smuggled from house to house, farm to farm, his location changing every few weeks or months, young Samuel survived the war. As the Vittali's were involved with the Dutch Resistance, Samuel was even hidden for two weeks in their household, playing and sleeping in the same room with his seven-year-old cousin, Joe (my uncle) before disappearing entirely with the help of the underground. When grown men, this brief moment of mutual childhood was remembered vividly by each.

Samuel's grandparents, Henri and Engeltje Kattenburg, were hauled via freight-train to Auschwitz, a three-day journey, sometimes four if the train was ordered to stop to allow more important trains to pass. Over 100 people would be locked into these train cars with only one or two buckets serving as toilets, and, maybe, one bucket of drinking water.

With virtually no ventilation, no windows, and reeking of sweat, urine, vomit, and excrement, the confined, dark swaying space became overwhelmingly sickening in a matter of hours. No food was provided. Sitting or lying down with any level of comfort was impossible, and after the first day, all shreds of human dignity disintegrated.

Children whined from hunger and fear, babies cried incessantly, mothers wept in angry frustration, and men were explosive with rage. The ill or elderly often did not survive the journey and would be found lying dead as the living grappled with the horror they found themselves in, a grim foreshadowing of horrors soon to come.

The Kattenburgs were gassed immediately upon arrival at Auschwitz on July 16, 1943. Henri was fifty-four and Engeltje fifty-five. Both were in the prime of their lives. Samuel's parents were likewise deported to

Auschwitz, but much later, on September 7, 1943. They were forced into hard labour. Some months afterward, Samuel's mother, Mathilda, was transported from Auschwitz to the Bergen-Belsen concentration camp, where she died on April 14, 1944, at the age of thirty-one.

Samuel's father, Levie, was marched from Auschwitz to Poland as part of a group of slave workers sent to clean up after the destruction of the Polish Ghetto in Warsaw. He died somewhere in Central Europe on July 1, 1944. He was forty years old.

When the war ended and Holland was liberated from the Germans, it took years to reunite the children who had been hidden, like Samuel, with any remaining families, or to locate distant relatives. Most of the children were orphaned, but for those who were not, often when a surviving relative was found, Dutch families refused to give up their charges, having taken them in as babies and now wishing to keep them as their own. Children did not recognize returning parents, and parents finally reuniting with their children after gaps of four or more years, were rejected as strangers.

Samuel and I have another cousin who survived solely by her parent's sacrificial willingness to hide her. She, at only seven-months old, was given away to the Resistance and hidden on a Dutch farm, blending in with that family's existing children. Like Samuel, she was an only child. And like Samuel, both her parents were killed. Her new Dutch parents kept her, raised her, and loved her as if she was their own daughter.

By 1946, records from the concentration camps, made public by the Red Cross, revealed that Samuel's parents and grandparents were killed at Auschwitz. His closest relative was his mother's brother, Andries Kattenburg, who had returned to New York City after having served in the US military in Europe, volunteering for duty when the United States entered the war.

Samuel—a little boy orphaned, traumatized, and displaced—at the mere age of seven was seated, alone, on a KLM flight from Amsterdam, with no money and unable to speak a word of English. He was flown to the United States and subsequently flown to Australia—a horrendous trip for a child. There, an aunt and uncle whom he had never met who had immigrated to Australia before the war, raised him.

Giovanni Vittali, true to his word, placed Henri Kattenburg's ƒ100,000 Dutch guilders (worth about $250,000 Canadian in 2021 dollars) into a savings account at *De Nederlandsche Bank* (DNB), the Dutch Central Bank. The bank, as was to become their precedent in similar situations, kept 100% of the money as payment and compensation for supposedly unpaid taxes owed by Mr. Kattenburg; rather difficult to file taxes after having been deported and murdered.

His surviving grandson, Samuel Wennek, who had lost everything, received nothing.

2018 - TORONTO

hat a privilege and honour to email back and forth with my seventy-nine-year-old second cousin, Samuel. He was living in Switzerland and sadly, widowed. A second cousin—miraculous—we shared the same great-grandparents. My Oma (Betje Vittali-Hijman) and his Oma (Engeltje Kattenburg-Hijman) were sisters.

Samuel explained that the *In Memoriam* section I discovered on the Coenraad Roed website which led me to him, was included at his request. He was the benefactor supporting the creation of that website. He also was the leading financial supporter for the book, *Saving the Children*, the story of how 600 Dutch Jewish children were spared from the Holocaust by the heroic efforts of employees of the daycare and nursery centre located across the street from the Schouwburg Theatre. These children were hidden in the homes, barns, basements, and attics of over 1,000 sympathetic Dutch families throughout the Netherlands. Samuel casually mentioned this book in passing in one of our email messages.

I acquired a copy of *Saving the Children* through Amazon. As I was reading, I came to realize this was Samuel's story, and understood the extreme sacrifice his parents made for him and for his future. It was also a story of the heart-wrenching emotional torture suffered by the parents of children who knew they might never see their child again. Newborns, toddlers, little ones under seven—all blindly handed over to the mercy of strangers. The book documents the extensive secretive plans, strategies, and heroic actions of individuals who risked their lives to save these children from what would have most certainly been a horrifying and tragic death.

In October 2018, Samuel let me know he was going to visit his family in New York and that afterwards, in early December, he would very much like to meet in Toronto, if I was amenable. Are you kidding? Absolutely! I would be thrilled.

So, plans were made that he would fly, and we would drive. Samuel would be staying at the Shangri-La Hotel in downtown Toronto. We would convene, sight unseen, in the lobby. We both stayed in touch leading up to our meeting date to make sure the weather and everyone's schedules cooperated.

After parking a few blocks away, off we went to find the Shangri-La on University Avenue. We found ourselves mildly lost trying to locate the appropriate public entrance, but eventually found our way in. Several lobby-like options existed, and we wandered around looking for any pseudo-elderly individual meeting Samuel's description.

I must admit, a few fleeting thoughts of the surrealism of the situation and its movie-like semblance to a psychological thriller crossed my mind. What if this all turned out horribly wrong, and we were heading straight into some kind of bizarre scam, or worse? Pushing such thoughts aside, I approached the front desk to inquire if Mr. Samuel Wennek had checked in and, if so, to alert him to our arrival.

I recognized him immediately. Something about meeting a new relative, no matter whether a newborn or full-grown adult, makes you search their face intently. Perhaps their gait, a smile, or their eyes remind you of others with those same features. Samuel was kind, gracious, humble, and generous, treating us to lunch and a glorious bottle of superb Italian wine coupled with a fabulous box of Swiss chocolates.

I brought along my copy of *Saving the Children,* and asked for his autograph, which he wrote, first name only —such a sweet, humble, and unassuming man. How proud his parents and grandparents would be to know that their young Samuel had grown up to be a truly remarkable person, forgive the cliché, against all odds.

On my laptop, I showed him pictures of my family, my mother's family, and relatives he never knew existed.

In turn, he showed me pictures of his family, and then explained the reason why he had taken such a long journey to the United States from Switzerland.

"Here is my son, Benjamin, and his wife, Jennifer," a lovely couple, young, happy, carefree, smiled at me from the streets of New York, "and their newborn twins, Asher and Saskia."

My jaw dropped, flabbergasted. "Samuel! Really? Twins? Your son has TWINS?" I could not hide my level of joy, disbelief, and delight. It was incredible. Phenomenal. After seventy-eight years, a bridge once collapsed, dismantled and buried, was now discovered and rebuilt for the future. Our eyes met in an elated expression of wonder! There we were, two distant relatives separated by countries and generations, language and tradition, and despite never having met before, now bonded by a past so meaningful, so rich.

"Twins run in the family, you know."

FACES & PLACES

$\mathcal{T}$he following, in chronological order, are mini-biographies of discovered family twins that were either killed or died during the Holocaust. All were related, most being first and second cousins to each other, and first (once removed), second, or third cousins, to me. We are all descendants of the same great-great, or great-great-great, grandparents.

It can be assumed that they knew each other, or, at the very least, knew of each other. Amsterdam was home—many living just a few short blocks away. And truly, they were just ordinary people. There was nothing to make them stand out as different—not their clothes, their speech, their jobs, or how they lived.

The Jewish line on my mother's side had been resident in Amsterdam for over 400 years. They fled religious persecution in Poland in the 1500s and travelled to the Netherlands, a country well known for its acceptance and tolerance of others.

Dutch Jews had wholly assimilated into Dutch society. They were shopkeepers, seamstresses, diamond cutters, butchers, flower sellers, bakers, leather workers, furniture makers, carpenters, factory workers, paper suppliers, bookbinders, cigar makers and even just poor peddlers. All of them, like all of us, worked hard to create a better life for their families and simply wished to live in peace.

Despite months of internet searching, the only photographs I found, of any of the discovered twins, were of the Bril sisters. The precious few other photographs I did find were of various related family members. They are included here to put faces to family names, and bring reality to dates and places cited. I do not know who has the original photographs, or how/where they were found, but my heart is filled with tremendous thanks to those individuals, wherever they are.

These few pictures stand as torchbearers for all the hundreds upon hundreds of missing photographs and stories that can never be found or known, strewn across abandoned floors, long swept away into dust—forgotten, unidentified, nameless.

The ages and dates are, each time, an emotional shock. The eye at first does not even see, let alone accept, the horrific truths the numbers expose. Mothers with all their young children around them all killed at the same time, or an elderly couple, obviously arrested and deported together, also murdered together. The gruesomeness and cruelty of it all is staggering and overwhelming.

Our twenty-first century educated minds grapple with how this could be, how it was, or the why of it. It is arrogant to think that any of us have the slightest understanding of what those last days and hours were like for those forced to endure them. What could a parent possibly say to console a child at such a time in such a place? The extreme level of terror and fear, confusion and disbelief, frustration and anger could not have been worse, nor can it be contained, understood, or explained in any meaningful way.

To the Nazis, the Jewish people, along with the Roma and Sinta (gypsies), Blacks, Jehovah's Witnesses, people with disabilities, and homosexuals were all less than human and therefore, needed to be exterminated, as if they were the bubonic plague personified or an infestation of cockroaches. You could not possibly allow such people to continue in society, to have families, to thrive, or, God forbid, marry outside their own communities, thus defiling the purity of the genetically superior Aryan race.

My grandmother's cloth Star of David badge; saved,
kept, and preserved by her youngest son.

"As Jewish and other "undesirables" were brought into the camp via train, they underwent a Selektion, or selection, on the ramp. Those deemed unfit for work were sent directly to the gas chambers. However, the Nazis kept this a secret and told the unsuspecting victims that they had to undress for a bath.

Led to a camouflaged gas chamber with fake shower-heads, the prisoners were trapped inside when a large door was sealed behind them. Then, an orderly, who wore a mask, opened a vent on the roof of the gas chamber and poured Zyklon B pellets down the shaft. He then closed the vent to seal the gas chamber.

The Zyklon B pellets turned immediately into a deadly gas. In a panic and gasping for air, prisoners would push, shove, and climb over each other to reach the door. But there was no way out. In five to 20 minutes, depending on the weather, all inside were dead from suffocation.

After it was determined that all had died, the poisonous air was pumped out, which took about 15 minutes. Once it was safe to go inside, the door was opened and a special unit of prisoners, known as the Sonderkommando, hosed down the gas chamber and used hooked poles to pry the dead bodies apart.

Rings were removed and gold plucked from teeth. Then the bodies were sent to the crematoria, where they were turned into ash."

— HTTPS://WWW.THOUGHTCO.COM/ ZYKLON-B-GAS-CHAMBER-POISON- 1779688

Nazi propaganda boasted of its mercy and humanity in allowing mothers and children, elderly husbands and wives, to remain together "to the end". They were of the absolute conviction that this scourge, these vast groups of people, had to be eliminated. It would be cruel to separate them. Look at how kind we are, how merciful and considerate, ensuring families are with each other, always.

Believing a thing, no matter how deep or ingrained that belief, does not miraculously transform it into a truth.

What is, is.

What anyone anywhere believes
does not, and cannot,
change what is.

TWINS *Flora and Schoontje Hoost* were born on October 20, 1868. They were the last two children of Roosje and Levie Hoost, who had three sons, and then the twin girls. Their father, Levie, was a diamond cutter and polisher in Amsterdam, a profession shared by many in the family.

Flora married and had three children, but was widowed in 1940. Her firstborn son, Benjamin, died tragically at only seven months old. In 1943 Flora was arrested, separated from her family, transported to Sobibor and killed on April 9.

Her daughter, Roosje, age forty-four, along with Roosje's husband, Hartog, age forty-seven, and daughter, Mary, age nineteen, were all killed at Auschwitz on January 31, 1944.

Flora and Schoontje's niece, Alida, with husband, Meindert, and son, Donald. Mother and son were killed in Auschwitz on June 11, 1943. Alida was only twenty-five and little Donald, just past two. Meindert died in Auschwitz on September 24, 1943.

Flora's third child, named Benjamin after a little brother who had died as a child, survived the war along with his wife, Gerardina, and four-year-old daughter, Florina.

Schoontje was widowed in 1932. She, along with her daughter, Clara, age fifty-two, were both killed at Auschwitz on September 28, 1943.

Schoontje's youngest children, Levie and Rosa, died in Sobibor on June 11, 1943, ages fifty and forty-five respectively. Schoontje's eldest son, Salomon, died in Auschwitz on October 5, 1942, age fifty-three.

Flora and Schoontje never lived more than five minutes away from each other their entire lives. They were seventy-three years old when they died, the eldest in our long line of Holocaust family twins.

TWINS *ABRAHAM and Isaac de Vries* were born on November 16, 1890, the third-born children of Salomon and Leentje de Vries. Their father was a simple peddler. The family had four sons and two girls in addition to the twins, making a large family of eight children. The twins' mother, Leentje, had siblings that were stillborn twins in 1864, and Leentje's sister had twins as well!

Abraham never married. He died in Auschwitz on September 30, 1942, age fifty-one.

Isaac was a successful and respected shopkeeper in Amsterdam. He married and had two children. Isaac died in Auschwitz on November 5, 1942, age fifty-one.

Were these brothers at Auschwitz at the same time? They had to have been. Did Isaac know that his twin brother, Abraham, was dead? He had to have. What he did not know, though, was what was going to happen to his wife, son, daughters and granddaughter.

Isaac and Abraham's sister, Mietje de Vries-de Haan; killed at Sobibor, July 9, 1943, age fifty.

Isaac's wife, Debora, age fifty, along with their daughter, Lena, age twenty-six, were both gassed in Auschwitz on August 3, 1943. Isaac's son, Salomon, died in Auschwitz on April 30, 1943, at age twenty-seven. Salomon's wife, Rachael, and three-year-old daughter, Flora (Isaac's granddaughter), had been killed previously on February 1, 1943. It is very possible that Isaac had been selected for slave labour at Auschwitz and died from either disease, exhaustion or starvation. Isaac's youngest daughter, Marianne, is on record as having been deported to Westerbork on March 10, 1942, and ultimately survived the war.

Isaac and Abraham's little niece, Rebecca, pictured below, was killed at Sobibor on July 2, 1943, when she was just ten years old, along with her mother and father.

This photo was most likely taken at the famous Zaandvoort beach just outside of Amsterdam. Look at the adorable little mini shade-houses, and people all set up to enjoy a day at the beach, complete with tables and actual china. Notice the joined, tall houses in the background with their unique gables so characteristic of Amsterdam —such a sweet photo representing happier, innocent times.

MY FATHER'S GRANDMOTHER, my great-grandmother, had a beautiful heritage home on the Zaandvoort beach, and operated it as a highly successful Bed & Breakfast Inn and boarding house. My father vividly remembers being with his Oma almost every weekend in the summers, playing in the sand in front of her home.

When the Nazis occupied the Netherlands, they confiscated my great-grandmother's home due to its prime location on the ocean. She was forced to move in with her eldest daughter, my grandmother, into the house on the Amsteldijk, the house adjoining the Vittali's. Her beautiful, ancient home on the beach was destroyed during the war. With her house and business gone, my great-grandmother lost everything she had.

On September 15, 1941, Dutch Jews were barred from public parks, zoos, cafes, bars, restaurants, hotels, sleeping and dining cars on trains, theatres, concerts, public libraries and museums, sporting events, beaches, and swimming pools.

Taxis, private cars, and bicycles were forbidden. Travel on any public transportation required special permits not easily obtained, and even then, Jews had to travel in the lowest class, and could not sit down until all non-Jews had found seats. They were not permitted to have telephones, or use public phones. They could not buy fruit; vegetables only could be purchased at particular Jewish stores (where supplies were pitiful).

Jews were forbidden to sit on public benches, play sports in public, or even walk on the sunny side of a street. They could not visit any non-Jewish homes. All Jews had to be inside from 8 p.m. until 6 a.m. During these hours, they could not lean out of a window or sit on a front balcony or yard. All windows had to be shut.

By the late fall of 1941, all employed Jews had lost their jobs and, except at Jewish-owned businesses, were deemed unemployable. The vast majority of the Jewish population was stripped of all rights, marginalized, and impoverished within a matter of weeks. This extensive community of respected law-abiding and tax-paying Dutch citizens first figuratively disappeared within the country, then literally disappeared out of the country.

Although there were written protests from churches, some government officials and the absent monarchy, these were summarily ignored. The Germans had replaced the existing Dutch government with their own occupying government. Therefore, the bulk of power in the Netherlands rested in Nazi hands.

With the help of the Dutch police, on February 12, 1941, German soldiers cordoned off old Amsterdam Jewish neighbourhoods, encircling them with barbed wire, installing police checkpoints, and opening the bridges over canals, effectively cutting off residents from the rest of the city.

One week later, a fight broke out between Jewish citizens and German soldiers in the Koko ice-cream shop, and several soldiers were injured. In response, the Nazis brutally tightened restrictions on Dutch Jews.

Driving their supremacy home, the occupying forces rounded up 425 young Jewish men and deported them to Buchenwald and Mauthausen, including three of my direct relatives. Of these 425 men, only two ultimately survived; all the others died within a year, my relatives included.

On February 25, 1941, over 300,000 Dutch workers went on a two-day strike to protest this overt persecution of their Jewish friends and neighbours by the German occupiers. The strike was suppressed by the police, but it stands as the only nation-wide public outcry against the treatment of Jews by any country in all of Europe. My aunt, Christina, speaks of this strike in her personal diary, and how upon arriving to work, she and all the other workers were sent home for three days. Also showing solidarity, her father's construction business also shut down work during that time.

After the failure of the strike, there were no more publicly organized demonstrations or complaints; any and all future action against the occupying Germans moved underground to the hidden realm of rising Dutch Resistance groups.

As the Jewish population, for centuries an integral part of the fabric of the Netherlands, Amsterdam in particular, was pushed further and further out of everyday life, *out of sight* became, sadly, *out of mind*.

∾

TWIN GIRLS, ***Engeltje and Matje Kool***, were born on September 2, 1894, to Elias and Elisabeth Kool. This large family had seven girls and two boys, including the twin girls. One of the twins, **Matje**, died just before her fourth birthday. Elias's occupation is not known. He died in 1920 leaving Elisabeth a widow with two young girls still at home.

Engeltje, the surviving twin, married and had two sons. She and her husband, Joseph, were both gassed on October 12, 1942, in Auschwitz. Engeltje was forty-eight and Joseph was fifty-eight.

Joseph Kool, Engeltje and Matje's oldest brother, and the father of the twins, Isaac and Elie Kool. Joseph died in Auschwitz on February 28, 1943, at the age of fifty.

Their sons survived as manual labourers at Auschwitz for awhile, but Meier, the eldest son, died at age twenty-seven on January 5, 1943, while his younger brother, Elias, died shortly thereafter at age twenty-five on April 30, 1943.

Engeltje's brother, Salomon, was the father of the twins Isaac and Elie Kool, born in 1922—no doubt these younger family twins had a great relationship with their aunt Engeltje.

The eight surviving Kool children were all grown with

families of their own by 1940, but not a single member of the family survived.

Their grandmother, Elisabeth, was also killed. She had remarried after her first husband died. She and her second husband were arrested and deported together, and gassed in Auschwitz on March 13, 1943, both at the age of seventy-five.

～

TWINS *JOSEPH and Sarah Judels* were born on May 22, 1895, to Lion and Schoontje Judels. The family had seven boys and five girls, including the fraternal twins. The last child born, a boy, died at age five in 1919. Lion was a furniture maker. Joseph and Sarah were aunt and uncle to the Zwaaf twins born in 1940, Mozes and Eva.

Joseph, his wife, Mietje, and their two children, Sarah and Lion, were all gassed on July 2, 1943, at Sobibor. Their eldest daughter, Schoontje, also died at Sobibor on May 28, 1943, at age seventeen. Joseph was forty-eight, Mietje was forty-six, Sarah was fourteen, and Lion was twelve.

Nothing is known about what happened to Joseph's twin sister, **Sarah**, but it can be assumed that she died somewhere in Europe during the Holocaust. The entire Judels' large, extended family, which, by 1940, had grown to include spouses, children and grandchildren, siblings of spouses and their families, was very, very extensive. The family was eliminated entirely except for two brothers, who, along with their wives, managed to survive.

Alexander Judels, Joseph and Sarah's older brother, joined the Hollandia-Kattenburg textile and sewing factory on February 1, 1927. Mr. Henri Hyman Kattenburg, Samuel Wennek's grandfather, was one of the factory owners, a well known businessman and direct family relative who employed many family and non-family individuals in their factories.

Without warning, on Wednesday, November 11, 1942, at around 4:30 p.m., there was a sudden *Sicherheitspolizei* (German security police) raid on the Kattenburg factories.

All exits were blocked, and the Jewish workers, mostly young, single women and young married men who could not get employment elsewhere, were aggressively separated out, catalogued as per required Nazi reporting, and hauled away. True to form, the German SS kept a photographic record of these "arrested" workers, not only those of that evening, but all others previously rounded up in similar raids. Individuals removed had no opportunity to advise their families, gather any belongings, or say any goodbyes.

After being forcibly taken, they were transported to Westerbork, and ultimately deported to the concentration camps in Poland, Germany, and Austria.

That morning, like every morning, these bright young people would have had their breakfast, tossed back their coffee, kissed husbands, wives, children, or parents goodbye, and left for work.

Who could have guessed that by evening they would be gone, very likely never seen or heard from, or about, ever again.

Photograph of of Alexander Judels taken by German Security during a raid on the Hollandia-Kattenburg factory. He has a defiant look in his eye!

TWINS *SAMUEL and Gerrit Rabbie* were born on October 31, 1903, to Jacob and Marianne Rabbie, and into their family of all boys, the twins being their last born children. Jacob owned a diamond processing company, and **Samuel**, who worked in his father's diamond business, never married. He lived with his elderly parents until he was arrested by the Germans and deported. Separated from his family and parents, Samuel died in Sobibor on April 30, 1943, at the age of thirty-nine. Samuel and Gerrit's parents were gassed in Auschwitz on December 3, 1942. Jacob was seventy-four, and Marianne was sixty-nine.

Gerrit, who worked as a paper wholesaler, survived the war and passed away in the Netherlands in his seventy-fifth year. He and his wife, Margaretha, were transported to Terezin, a concentration camp thirty miles north of Prague in the Czech Republic. As they had no children, they worked as slave labourers and miraculously, both survived.

The other boys of the family also survived the war. This was either due to some being successfully hidden by the Dutch Resistance, escaping to Switzerland, or being of sufficient strength and endurance to survive the gruelling labour of the concentration camps. The boys were of the correct age to be chosen for hard work instead of being selected for the gas chambers.

The following is the only family photograph I was able to find of anyone in the Rabbie family. It is of a nephew of Samuel and Gerrit's, young Maurits Druijff, born July 17, 1935.

Seven-year-old Maurits. Gassed at Sobibor with his father, Meijer, thirty-five, his mother, Mirjam, thirty-nine, and baby sister, Beatrix, age four, on June 11, 1943.

TWINS *SIMON and Femma Snoek* were born on September 24, 1914, the last-born children of Mozes and Engeltje Snoek. Mozes was a worker of some kind, most likely in a factory or shipyard. Little **Simon** died just before his first birthday on September 14, 1915. The Snoek family suffered much sorrow, with three of their seven children dying in infancy, and one son dying at the age of twenty-two.

Femma, the twin that lived, was named after a younger sister, also named Femma, who had died when only five months old. This was a prevalent Dutch practice —naming a subsequent child after an earlier child that did not live.

The rest of the family were all killed; the twins' parents on April 2, 1943, and thirty-year-old sister Elisabeth, along with her four-year-old son, Jacob, on September 21, 1942, all at Auschwitz.

Femma and her husband, Hijman, were gassed together on September 30, 1942, also in Auschwitz just eight days after her sister, Elisabeth. Femma and Simon's oldest brother, Ephraim, endured the tortures of concentration camp life the longest. He died on March 31, 1944, at an unknown location in Central Europe.

Ephraim's wife, Henriette, along with their two daughters, Sophia and Engelina, survived the war.

Mother and daughters must have been separated from each other and hidden by the Dutch Resistance, as if they had been deported to a concentration camp, a young mother with two small children had absolutely no hope of survival.

The Snoek twins' aunt and uncle on their wedding day, May 23, 1934. Henriette and her two daughters were some of the very few who survived. Ephraim sports a fancy satin top hat and gloves. Notice the lovely delicate head-piece on Henriette's veil.

~

TWINS *BETTY and Rachel Casoeto* were born on July 16, 1916, to Mozes and Esther Casoeto. Their brother, Abraham, was five years old when his twin sisters were born. Mozes worked as a diamond cutter and Esther as a seamstress.

The entire family died at Auschwitz. Betty was gassed on September 30, 1942, and Rachel died on November 11, 1942, most likely from either gassing, starvation or disease. The twins were just past their 26th birthday. As was so common, their older parents were gassed upon arriving at Auschwitz on February 26, 1943. Their brother, Abraham, survived the longest, living until March 13, 1943.

Remarkably, the Casoeto's extended family's story did not end in tragedy and suffering. The twins' grandfather, one uncle, one aunt and two cousins all survived the war along with all their spouses and children. How I wish I could unearth their stories!

The Dutch Jewish Monument records that the Casoeto family had a Lira bank account, the total value of which would have been confiscated at the time of their deportation. Unless an immediate family member whose name was on the account returned to claim the money, their bank funds, like the funds of so many others, a cumulative amount in the millions of dollars, would simply have been kept. The Dutch banking system enriched itself greatly at the cost of the lives of many.

Sadly, I could not locate photos of any member of the Casoeto family.

~

Twins *Isaac and Elie Kool*, the eldest sons of Joseph and Debora Kool, were born on May 15, 1922. Two more boys were born in subsequent years. Their father, Joseph, was a worker in either a factory or a shipyard.

The entire extended Kool family was killed in the Holocaust, including Joseph's mother, Elisabeth—the twins' grandmother—who was the mother of twins herself (Engeltje and Matje Kool mentioned earlier). Joseph's sister, Marianne, was married to my grandmother's brother, Benjamin, and was the mother of little Stella whose name I saw on that first list years ago.

Isaac and his wife, Isabella, along with Isaac's younger brother, Salomon, age seventeen, were all gassed on September 30, 1942, in Auschwitz. Isaac and Isabella were only twenty years old.

Elie was one of the 425 young Jewish men deported in February, 1941, the event sparking the Dutch Worker's Strike a few days later. Elie died in Mauthausen, Austria, on September 22, 1941, age nineteen. His parents most likely had no idea that he was dead or even where he had been taken.

The Kool twin's littlest brother, Lion, age nine, died along with his mother, Debora, age forty-nine, on October 22, 1942, in Auschwitz.

The twins' uncle was my great-uncle, Benjamin Hijman, married to Marianne Kool. Together they had four girls and one boy.

Marianne, age forty-one, and her three daughters, Leisje, twelve, Engeltje, nine, and Stella, seven, were gassed together at Auschwitz on November 19, 1942. Roza, their eldest child, age twenty, was gassed along with her husband, Nathan, age twenty-three, on May 21, 1943, in Sobibor.

The photo on the previous page is adorable Stella Hijman, one of my mother's numerous first cousins. There is a tiny bit of a girl visible beside Stella, whose top is the same style and material as hers. This is possibly her first cousin, Esther Engeltje Arons, named after Benjamin's sister, Engeltje, Samuel Wennek's grandmother. These two little girls were only three months apart in age. Although very blonde, It could also be Stella's younger sister, another Engeltje, who was two years younger than Stella.

Elias Hijman, Benjamin and Marianne's only son, died in Auschwitz on August 16, 1942, at age seventeen, three months before his mother and sisters. He would have been old enough to have been chosen as a worker instead of killed outright, but perhaps not strong enough to survive the extreme hardship and constant lack of food. His father, Benjamin, survived the horrors of concentration camp the longest, dying on February 29, 1944, somewhere in Central Europe, the exact place unknown.

Benjamin Hijman, Stella's father and my grandmother's youngest brother.

Marianne Hijman-Kool, the Kool twins' and my mother's, aunt.

TWINS *ALEX AND FLORA VAN DER SLUIJS* WERE BORN ON OCTOBER 28, 1928, to Izak and Regina van der Sluijs. Izak was a highly respected shop owner.

They had five children: three boys and two girls, including the fraternal twins. At age fourteen, **Alex** and **Flora** were gassed on February 1, 1943, along with their parents and older brother, Eduard, age sixteen, all at Auschwitz. Izak was fifty-five and Regina fifty-one when they were killed.

Izak van der Sluijs

Regina van der Sluijs-Pels

The twins' oldest brother, Arend, died on March 31, 1944, somewhere in Central Europe at a place unknown. He was thirty-one years old. Arend's wife, Sara, age thirty-one, along with their six-year-old daughter, Regina, named after her grandmother, were gassed at Sobibor, July 23, 1943.

Arend and Sara's youngest daughter, Roosje, at barely

two years old, had been taken from her parents and died at the Herzogenbusch concentration camp, a Nazi camp located in Vught near the town of Hertogenbosch, the Netherlands.

The twins' remaining sister, Greta, married outside the Jewish community, and therefore escaped Nazi deportation.

~

TWINS *Louie and Theo Mossel* were born on March 11, 1928, the second set of twins born to Alexander and Henriette Mossel. Alexander was a skilled bookbinder and respected book dealer.

The Mossels had an extensive family of five girls and eight boys. The entire family, except for one of the twins, **Louie**, was murdered in the Holocaust. Louie was ill and in the hospital when the particularly brutal razzia that took his family occurred. Upon being released, he found everyone gone. Louie went into hiding for the remainder of the war. He never married.

Louie and Theo's mother, and youngest sister, Reana.

The remaining Mossel family was, over two years, forcibly deported, divided and dispersed between the camps of Auschwitz and Sobibor. The precise details of their stories are a mystery.

Reana, age ten, the Mossel twins' youngest sister, did not die on the same date as, or with, anyone else in her family. She was in a boarding school for disabled and difficult to educate children. The entire school was raided the night of January 21, 1943, and all students, teachers and administrators were taken, put on cattle cars, and sent to Auschwitz.

On May 21, 1943, twin **Theo**, age fifteen, along with his two younger brothers and parents, was murdered at Sobibor.

Particularly tragic is the fate of the twins' sister, Betsy's, little one-year-old boy, Joseph. He died on January 28, 1944, yet his parents died much earlier in March and April of 1943. Where was this wee one hiding? Who was taking care of him? Was he betrayed? It is impossible to know and more impossible to imagine.

| *The Mossel twins' eldest sister, Betsy.*

～

Twins *MAURITS AND MAX RIMINI* WERE BORN ON DECEMBER 11, 1928, to Jechiel and Lea Rimini (Wijnschenk). They were the middle children, an elder brother and younger brother completing the family. Jechiel, along with his father and brothers, were fishmongers, and Jechiel was the chief warehouse manager of the fishery in Amsterdam. The Wijnschenk family, over a number of generations, had many sets of multiple births.

The entire family died at Auschwitz. Lea, age forty-three, the twins, age thirteen, along with their younger brother, Sal, age seven, were all gassed on November 23, 1942. Their father, Jechiel, age forty-four, and the twins' oldest brother, Emanuel, age fifteen, both died a few months later on February 28, 1943.

Maurits and Max had eight first-cousins all very close in age. This extended family, from the grandfather to the grandchildren, including all spouses and siblings, died in the Holocaust. Except for Lea and her youngest boys, who were gassed immediately upon arriving at Auschwitz, it appears that the other cousins, due to their age, were selected for slave labour and most likely died from exhaustion, starvation, disease, or were killed outright.

Jechiel Roselaar, the Rimini twins' eldest first cousin. Killed at Sobibor on May 23, 1943, age twenty-two.

∿

TWINS *KLAARTJE AND MARGARETHA (GREETJE) BRIL* WERE BORN ON JANUARY 9, 1931 to Barend and Christina Bril (Hijman). Christina, their mother, was one of my grandmother's second cousins. These twins lived almost next door to the van Cleef twins, Eddy and Jochem—more family living so very close to each other, and no doubt involved in each other's lives.

The girls, who were identical twins, had one older brother, and a baby sister. Another sibling died in infancy in 1934. Their father, Barend, was a carpenter. He survived the Auschwitz concentration camp and lived to be 93. The twins' older brother, whose name is unknown, also survived!

The twins, age twelve, their little sister, Helena, age four, and their mother, Christina, age thirty-six, all died in Auschwitz on November 19, 1943. Christina's elderly parents, as well as her three sisters and their families, were killed the year before. Christina's brother, Salomon, who married a non-Jewish girl, was arrested, incarcerated, and deported, but survived the war.

This picture of Klaartje and Greetje is the only surviving photograph of any of our family's Holocaust twins. I discovered it online in April, 2021, almost five years after I began unravelling the threads of our family's past.

Twins Klaartje and Margaretha Bril with their younger brother, who survived the Holocaust. The girls were three years older than my mother, and were among her many cousins. They lived a mere fifteen minute walk away from my mother's house.

TWINS *EDDY AND JOCHEM VAN CLEEF* WERE BORN ON APRIL 11, 1939, to Joel and Mirjam van Cleef. Mirjam came from the Spreekmeester family, who had suffered a set of stillborn twins in 1864. Joel was a skilled leatherworker and artisan. Keeping things all in the family, his cousin, Jochem, married Mirjam's sister, Vogeltje.

Mirjam, age thirty-eight, and her three-year-old twin boys were gassed on July 23, 1942. Joel, age thirty-three, died a few months later on September 30, 1942. They were all in Auschwitz.

The Spreekmaster and van Cleef families were very extensive. They suffered the same fate as countless other Dutch Jewish families with little possibility of escape and few exceptions to being rounded up, or forcibly arrested, and deported.

Out of over 100 members in both the Spreekmeester and van Cleef families, only eight survived. With so many of them at both Auschwitz and Sobibor, they must have had contact with each other as best they could while at the camps. They could not have helped but see the decimation of their family, the how and when of it, from the littlest baby to the oldest grandmother.

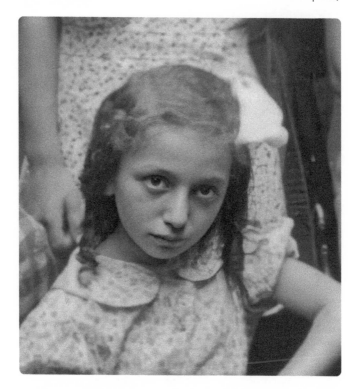

This photograph is of Floor (Flooretje, or little flower) Spreekmeester, one of the van Cleef twins' cousins. Little Rebecca Goudeket was also their cousin, as were the de Vries twins. Floor was killed in Auschwitz at the age of eleven on December 11, 1942, along with her parents: Jacob, age forty-seven, and Esther, forty-six.

Notice that Floor has the exact same dress fabric as the girl behind her, who was very likely a cousin. Floor was the only girl in her family, but had several cousins all around the same age.

Not long after the German occupation of Holland, oppressive restrictions on the Jewish population came into effect, including the removal of all Jewish children from public schools.

This larger picture above, only identified as a *photograph of Dutch school children, September 5, 1931,* did not have the place, date, names of children (other than Floor) or the teacher identified.

～

TWINS *TOBIAS and Abraham Hakker* were born on August 23, 1940, only three months after the invasion of Holland.

The twins were the last-born children of Salomon and Elisabeth Hacker. The couple had three older boys and one older girl. Salomon helped manage his father's fruit and vegetable market and butcher shop. As a separate business of his own, he crafted cigars. Based on the list of their looted family possessions, they were reasonably well off.

This entire family was annihilated. The three older boys were separated from their parents and siblings, and deported eight months before the rest of the family. Mozes, age twenty-one, Jaques, age nineteen, and Harry, age sixteen, were all killed at Sobibor on September 30, 1942.

The twins, barely over two years old, along with their older sister, Helena, age eleven, and their parents, age forty-four and forty-three, were gassed at Auschwitz on June 11, 1943. Salomon, the twins' father, was one of seven in his family, who were, of course, all married with their own families during these appalling times. None survived.

Celine van Cleef-Hakker and Louis Hakker, relatives of the Hakker and van Cleef twins. They died at Sobibor on July 16, 1943. They were both only twenty-one years old.

Twins *Mozes and Eva Zwaaf* were born on September 23, 1940, exactly one month after the birth of the Hakker twins who lived, literally, around the corner. Mozes and

Eva were the only children of Jacob and Helena Zwaaf. As noted previously, the Judels twins were also the cousins of the Zwaaf twins.

Helena was killed along with her children on September 14, 1942, shortly after her thirty-first birthday, the twins being not even two years old. Jacob, eight years younger than his wife, survived the Buchenwald concentration camp and immigrated to California after the war ended. His eight brothers and sisters, their spouses and children, plus both his parents, were killed. **Eva** and **Mozes** were the youngest of our family's Holocaust twins.

They had a baby cousin, Bernard, born to Helena's sister, Sientje on May 21, 1943, during the worst of the Jewish raids and deportations.

This little one died on August 7, 1943, at not even three months of age while being retained at the Westerbork concentration camp. Westerbork was a holding camp where tens of thousands of Dutch Jews were housed until there was "room" at the Polish, German, and Austrian camps. Baby Bernard's young mother, Sientje, at only twenty-seven years old, died in Auschwitz on September 24, 1943, together with her two remaining children, Salomon and Eva, ages nine and seven, just seven weeks after the loss of her infant son.

Sientje's husband, Hartog, died at Auschwitz four months after his wife and children, and two days after his twenty-ninth birthday. The heartache he must have suffered knowing his family had been murdered in the very place he was forced to labour in, is unfathomable.

Flora Stad, Helena Zwaaf's sister, and aunt of the Zwaaf twins. Flora died on June 4, 1943, at Sobibor, age twenty-nine.

The sobering, unmitigated events, and far-reaching invasiveness of the atrocity that was the Holocaust can never be reiterated enough. Its existence must continue to be told to all existing and future generations.

IN PLAIN SIGHT

The little Hakker twins were the first ones I discovered. I was not looking for twins in particular. I had forgotten my mother's remark of almost forty years ago. Their dates originally did not register with me as any different from all the other tragic dates.

But on a deeper look, something unexpected caught me by surprise, riveting me into paying closer attention. Two babies. Same date. Same year. In a split second I realized what was in front of me—a set of twins, in the family, just as my mother had said.

I began hunting through the data again, this time with a different view and purpose. And there they all were—first the one set, then two, three, four, five, and so many more—popping off the screen, out of hiding, right before my eyes.

Two dates, in particular, recur repeatedly. At first, hidden amongst so many others, they didn't stand out as unusual. Over time, however, they occurred too frequently to ignore. A broader investigation revealed a black tragedy to add to already heart-wrenching tragedies.

September 30, 1942

What an unimaginably heinous day. 103 family members murdered at Auschwitz, all at the same time. The youngest was fifteen years old, and the oldest, fifty-four. There were forty-six young people all under the age of twenty.

June 11, 1943

Another gruesome day—sixty-four family members gassed at Sobibor, 2 years old to 68 years old.

MY MIND IS FORCED to envision members of my family frantically trying to find each other amongst the over 2,000 souls in the gas chambers with no one knowing why they are there, or what is going to happen. Everyone stripped naked; parents displayed before the eyes of their children, and aged grandparents, in shame, weeping in their humiliation.

The doors are locked from the outside. Terror and realization set in when, instead of fresh water streaming from the shower-heads, poisonous, deadly gas exudes from vents in the ceiling. Helpless prisoners working just outside hear the screams of ensuing hysteria. There is no escaping these sounds of horror, or the tragedy, just as there is no escape for those trapped inside. Twenty minutes later, the deafening cacophony of death has gradually decayed into silence.

Bodies are splayed on the floor in a pile four feet high, spilling out the door when finally opened again. Gold teeth are yanked out. Hair is shaved off and sold at a profit to German processing plants where it was casually incorporated into products for military and everyday use.

Did families, immediate and extended, lay together in groups?

When everything is gone, but you still have those you love by your side, you cherish and hold on to them to the bitter end. The young family of one of my great-great-uncles was all gassed at Auschwitz on February 1, 1943: his wife, Rachel, age thirty-four, and her five children, aged nine, seven, five, three, and one year old. Which child died in her arms first, and which last?

Who forced the innocent at gunpoint into these chambers of horror? Who opened the canisters of Zyklon B pellets and poured them into the vents? Who was responsible for securing death with the locking of the doors?

An unexpected shock to modern-day tourists visiting Auschwitz are the still visible claw marks of human fingernails on the walls of the gas chambers.

My step-daughter married a German. A handsome, kind, fun-loving fellow. His grandparents were young adults in 1939. Where were they? What did they know? Did they have any level of involvement in the goings on within their native country?

No one knows. His grandfather committed suicide by shooting himself in the head at the end of the war.

Every family has their secrets.

≈

My family's Holocaust record displays a macabre list of lives taken, continuously and without pause except, and I note this with bitter irony, between December 17 and December 30 of each year: 1942, 1943, and 1944.

The Twins of Joseph Mengele

The most demonic butcher at Auschwitz was Dr. Joseph Mengele. He dissected people as if they were no more than frogs. Possessing a macabre fascination with twins, he believed they held some undiscovered genetic key, some possible clue leading to a new era of forced evolution via technological means. He was driven to attempt to manipulate and predict preferred citizens designed for a pure, future Aryan race.

Not wanting to know, but needing to know, I researched the lists of Mengele Twins, now publicly available. None of our family were on that list as most had been deported and killed before Mengele began his murderous experimentations. Small comfort.

Between 1864 and 1922, there were seven additional sets of twins born within the family. They were either stillborn, or did not survive infancy. Every single one of their immediate families were destroyed by the Holocaust. There is no doubt that had any of these twins lived, they too would have suffered the same fate as their grandparents, parents, brothers and sisters, cousins, aunts and uncles, nieces and nephews.

The tremendous sorrow, pain, and trauma of stillborn twins, or the loss of children very early in their lives surely, was reflected upon as a merciful blessing by their families during the war years.

Those tiny ones, who never experienced a single breath or the beauty and wonder of life, also never experienced the demonic side of humanity where so few in power could terrorize and torture so many so effortlessly.

GENERATIONS

$\mathcal{T}$he number of related family twins born from 1832 to 1942 is astounding. The average statistic in the Netherlands between 1900 and 1940 was thirteen twin births out of every 1,000 births. Our family, during that same time period, had fifteen sets out of approximately 550 births, more than double the national average.

After a seventy-eight-year glaring, gaping hole in our family line, that new set of twins born in 2018, the grandchildren of Samuel Wennek and my little second cousins one removed, are direct descendants of all those that lived before.

Bravo! Encore!

It seems rather apparent that we have, most definitely, a genetic disposition to multiple births.

In other words, "Twins run in the family, you know."

The Family Twins - 1720 to 2018

1. Joseph and Judith van Cleef; 1720
1st cousins, seven times removed
Ancestors of the 1939 van Cleef twins
Joseph died in 1790. Judith's death date is unknown.

2. Mozes and Salomon Hakker; 1787
3rd cousins, five times removed
ancestors of the 1940 Hakker twins
Mozes died in 1846, Salomon in 1873.

3. Hartog and Elkan Hakker; 1832
4th cousins, four times removed
twin sons of Salomon Hakker above
Death dates for both are unknown.

4. Klaartje and Rachel van Kollem; 1821
1st cousins, four times removed
Rachel lived only 19 days, Klaartje died in 1908.

5. Gerson, Betje and Gerrit Wijnschenk; 1840
my great-grandmother's uncles and aunt
Gerson died in 1903.
Death dates for Betje and Gerrit are unknown.

6. Joseph and Mordechai Reens; 1851
3rd cousins, once removed
Death dates for both are unknown.

7. Flora and Bloemetje Salomons; 1851
1st cousins, four times removed
great-aunts of the Mossel twins
Flora died in 1924. Bloemetje did not survive infancy.

8. Rachel and Frouke Salomons; 1852

1st cousins, four times removed
great-aunts of the Mossel twins
Both did not survive infancy.

9. Spreekmeester twins; 1864

2nd cousins, twice removed
stillborn

10. ***Flora and Schoontje Hoost; 1868

1st cousins, three times removed
Flora died in 1943, Schoontje in 1942.

11. Salomon and Sara Mechanicus; 1872

4th cousins, four times removed
Both did not survive infancy.

12. Lina and Joseph Stodel; 1880

1st cousins, four times removed
Both did not survive infancy or childhood

13. Wijnschenk twins; 1882

stillborn
related to the Wijnschenk triplets

14. ***Abraham and Isaac de Vries; 1890

2nd cousins, twice removed
Both died in 1942.

15. ***Engeltje and Matje Kool; 1894

great-uncle's sisters-in-law
Matje did not survive childhood.
Engeltje died in 1942.

16. ***Joseph and Sarah Judels; 1895
2nd cousins, three times removed
Joseph died in 1943. Sarah's date is unknown.

17. Jacob and Levie Mossel; 1899
2nd cousins, 3 times removed
Both did not survive infancy.

18. Vogeltje and Rebecca Serlui; 1901
2nd cousins, twice removed
Both did not survive infancy.

19. Betje and Heiman Kampion; 1902
3rd cousins twice removed
Both did not survive infancy.

20. Samuel and **Gerrit Rabbie; 1903
3rd cousins, once removed
Samuel died in 1943, Gerrit in 1978.

21. Simon and ***Femma Snoek; 1914
2nd cousins, once removed
Simon died as a baby in 1915. Femma died in 1942.

22. ***Betty and Rachel Casoeto; 1916
6th cousins
Both died in 1942.

23. ***Samuel and Jacob Stodel; 1917
1st cousins once removed
Jacob was stillborn. Samuel died in 1942.

24. Hillechiena and Harmanna Kampion; 1918
3rd cousins twice removed

Both did not survive infancy.

25. ***Isaac and Elie Kool; born 1922
1st cousins once removed
born eight days after the Mossel twins
Isaac died in 1942 and Elie in 1941.

26. **Louie and ***Theo Mossel; 1928
3rd cousins, twice removed
Theo died in 1942. Louie died in 2017.

27. ***Alexander, Flora van der Sluis; 1928
5th cousins, once removed
Both died in 1943, age 15.

28. ***Maurits and Max Rimini; 1928
related through the Wijnschenk family
Both died in 1942, age 14.

29. ***Klaartje and Margaretha Bril; 1931
1st cousins, five times removed
Both died in 1943, age 12.

30. ***Eddy and Jochem van Cleef; 1939
3rd cousins, once removed
Both died in 1942, age 3.

31. ***Tobias and Abraham Hakker; 1940
2nd cousins, once removed
Both died in 1943, age 2 1/2.

32. ***Eva and Mozes Zwaaf; 1940
2nd cousins, three times removed
Both died in 1942, two weeks before their 2nd birthday.

78 year gap

longest period of time with no twins in our family in over 200 years

32. Asher and Saskia Wennek; 2018

2nd cousins, once removed.
Asher has red hair like his great-grandfather.
Both alive and well!

** survived in hiding or at a concentration camp
*** died or were killed in the Holocaust

FACES & PLACES

$\mathcal{A}$t first, I had no pictures at all. None. Then, totally by surprise during one of my many geological searches, a photo of a distant lost relative appeared in someone else's family tree that they had matched to mine! I emailed the owner of the family tree with the photo, asked if we were related, and if so, how. I also asked how they had acquired this picture. A reply came back within a day and yes, we were related through marriage. The picture was located on joodsmonument.nl, a site I had not come across before.

This astonishing website, created as an online memorial to the tens of thousands of Dutch Jewish war victims, is a veritable trove of tragedy. With information added from government sources and private individuals, the site is an archive of almost every war-affected person —their families, where they lived, their occupation, who else lived at the same address at the time they were deported, a Google-earth picture of their home, any photos, a listing of possessions confiscated from their home, whether they had been forced to transfer their bank accounts to the "German looting bank"—basically, anything at all that was known about them including which concentration camp or other part of Europe they were deported to. All the family I had been researching blindly for were listed on this website, as well as a handful of rare and precious photographs.

Seeing the faces of direct family ancestors for the first time, even coupled with their tales of loss and tragedy, was miraculous and joyous, as if, somehow, I was bringing them back to life. Photographs create those poised moments in time, that split second of life, preserved, that supersedes even death.

My heart leapt in my throat when little Stella Hijman's picture appeared. Even my naturally romantic nature could not have imagined a sweeter child. How anyone could terrorize, abuse, and murder someone so precious is beyond comprehension. There exist no words strong enough or descriptive enough to depict the meticulously and methodically planned extermination of an entire race of people. Cruelty, bestiality, heinousness, demoniacal ... all these fall short. Barbarism lurks, restless and ever-present, under the thin skin of civilization, a mere scratch capable of rushing it oozing and festering to the surface.

Universally, people often treasure photos of their family almost above all else. In an emergency or natural disaster, photo albums are grabbed as if they are as necessary as bottled water.

Dutch Jews in hiding had only the clothes on their backs and perhaps a few cherished items. Those arrested and taken from their homes or during a raid had no opportunity to take anything with them at all. The obedient reporting at designated deportation stations were "allowed" to bring one piece of luggage each, no doubt containing family photographs. The luggage was a mere decoy, its contents confiscated, dumped, destroyed. Treasured pictures of babies and children, parents and grandparents, special days and every day—scattered, lost, gone.

The following photos were the only ones I could find of our family's children, victims of war killed for the "crime" of being born to parents, or even grandparents, who chose Judaism as their faith. These are the very faces of innocence, their dark, lovely almond-shaped eyes, so soft and expressive—wondering, waiting, hoping.

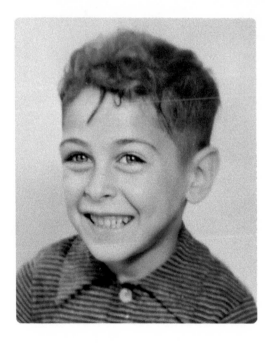

JOSHUA CROONENBERG, ABOVE, *was only seven years*

old when he was gassed at Sobibor on June 11, 1943, along with his father, Jacob, thirty-five, and mother, Elizabeth, thirty-four. Both sets of grandparents, his aunts, uncles, and cousins were all victims of the Holocaust.

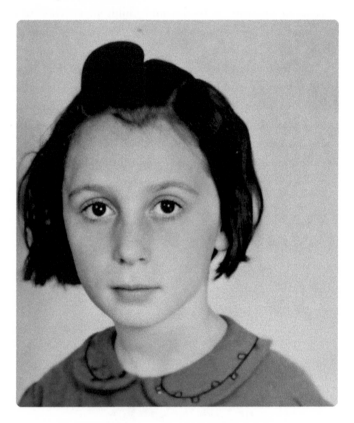

JETTY VAN KOLLEM *was the only child of Abraham and Elisabeth van Kollem. This family died at Sobibor on June 11, 1943. Jetty was eight, her mother, thirty, and her father, thirty-four.*

REINA VERDONER *was twelve when she was killed, along with her mother, Helena, age forty-two, at Auschwitz on March 12, 1943. Her father and grandfather had died a year earlier, and her uncle, aunt, and grandmother one month after her.*

CLARA FRANK *died at Auschwitz on February 15, 1944, at age eighteen. Her parents and older brother were already dead. Clara was alone. She was most likely a slave labourer and would have died from starvation, disease or exhaustion.*

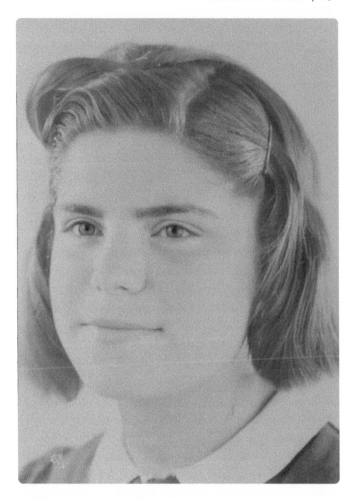

BETJE WAAS, AGE FIFTEEN, *was killed upon arrival at Auschwitz on September 29, 1942, along with both her parents, two younger sisters, and her younger brother; an entire family on the same day.*

MY MOTHER HAD a party at her home, Amsteldijk 46, for her fourteenth birthday in December, 1941. One present from her mother was a beautiful diary, bound in a homemade, black and white checkered cloth cover. The diary contained the typical blank pages for writing daily entries, but there were also pages for the autographs of friends and family.

There is an endearing entry, written carefully in beautiful hand-writing, by one of my mother's first cousins, fifteen-year-old Duifje "Dolly" Coppenhagen. Duifje's mother was one of my grandmother's younger sisters. My mother's diary with Duifje's sweet saying, is the only tangible surviving evidence that exists, along with the photograph of her and her grandparents below, to prove this young girl ever lived.

In this same diary are entries, dated in 1942, from two of my mother's aunts: Lea de Vries-Hijman and Mina Vittali-Tas. I have included these entries, translated into English, in the Translations section of this book.

Duifje, my mother, and a diary are written into Flora's birthday party story.

I often reflect on what immediate post-war life must have been like. The growing realization that all the playmate cousins your own age, all the admired older ones you envied and looked up to, all the adorable younger sets of twins you babysat—were brutally murdered.

How do you come to terms with that?

In reality, you don't.

∼

Duifje *died at Auschwitz, September 30, 1942, at age sixteen. Her parents, David, age forty, Henriette, thirty-nine, and brother, Louis, four, were gassed on July 2, 1943. Grandparents Johanna Duifje and Andries Coppenhagen (above) died on March 26, 1943.*

LEA HIJMAN, the youngest of the nine Hijman children, defied her Nazi deportation order, and went into hiding in the late summer of 1942, taking her eight-month-old son, Robert, with her. Her husband, Leo, was also in hiding.

There was a warrant out for Lea's arrest. She was charged with leaving her residence without proper authorization, the standard charge brought against any Jewish person that could not be located. For over two years, and constantly on the move, Lea and Leo were unable to see each other.

The Dutch Resistance made an arrangement for Lea and her son, along with a few others, to be smuggled out of Amsterdam, and then transported safely out of the country. She, somehow, was able to get a message to Leo, and they arranged to meet at the Rosicrucian Church where she was to liaise with those assisting in her escape.

On the arranged day, while waiting at the church, mother and son were caught in a sudden, unexpected razzia. Lea had been betrayed! From a short distance away, Leo could see what was happening.

In a desperate attempt to create a distraction for the Germans, and thus get Lea's attention so she could escape, he scaled the side of the church, yelling and waving his arms. Then, intentionally, he fell, breaking almost every bone in his body.

His spontaneous plan failed. Lea and their son, Robbie, did not escape. Leo survived the war in a Dutch insane asylum, pretending to be mentally deranged. After the liberation, refusing to accept the obvious, he searched for his lost wife and child for years.

Robert Julius de Vries *was killed at Auschwitz at age two, along with his mother, Lea, age thirty-five, on March 6, 1944. My sister, Leah, is named after her, and pudgy little Robert was one of Samuel Wennek's, and my mother's, many first cousins.*

Lea gave her wedding ring to Giovanni Vittali for safekeeping. It passed on to my mother, and my father passed it on to me after my mother died. I gave it to my son, Jonathan, when he became engaged, and his wife now wears it.

I used a number of details about Lea in my stories, even the references to cobblestones as seen in the above photograph.

REFLECTIONS

*H*ow is it possible that we still have a world where a group, any group, simply by the circumstance of geography, can consider itself superior and dominate another group? Does where we are born on this planet, which occurs entirely by chance, define us? How is it that others are so afraid of things they perceive as different from themselves? What is so threatening about an alternate view of the world beyond our own?

Racism, prejudice, and hatred don't ask such questions. That is why they still exist. As a child, I had no concept of racism, or even an awareness of the word. We are not born to hate, or be racist or prejudiced; these must be intentionally taught or exemplified in order to propagate.

Many Dutch citizens set aside assumptions or prejudices and muscled the strength and bravery to assist Dutch Jews. But it was not enough. One of the great tragedies of the extermination of Dutch Jewry was that it happened so easily, so methodically, and with such little impedance. The cumulative weekly deportations of hundreds of thousands of victims were supervised by a mere handful of SS soldiers, fewer than twenty in fact. There were, sadly, many Dutch people assisting and profiting from this mass exodus of humanity.

I've stood many times on the train platform at Union Station in Toronto, Canada's largest transportation hub. Once, while masses of unknown people pushed around me crowding into the train—faces blank, minds elsewhere—shivers ran down my spine. I stood, paralyzed, imagining ghosts from the past on another train, in another time.

The Dutch Railroad alone earned millions from the fares paid, or rather, extracted under duress. Railroad officials and employees were fully aware of the suffering played out in the freight cars they were transporting, and equally aware that the returning cars were always empty; no one had a two-way ticket.

Within hours of the arrest and removal of families, their homes were all too often broken into, and anything of value or use stolen by neighbours, without impunity. For a fee, conspiracists betrayed innocents, and for malice, neighbours betrayed neighbours.

The rest of the world was not unaware. As early as December 1942, leaked information coming from concentration camps and various Resistance Movements made the Allied governments of the United States, the United Kingdom and the Soviet Union aware that over 2,000,000 Jews had been exterminated and millions more were at risk. They did virtually nothing to assist.

There is shame in doing,
but also great shame in doing nothing.
The hunter, the hunted, and the watcher.

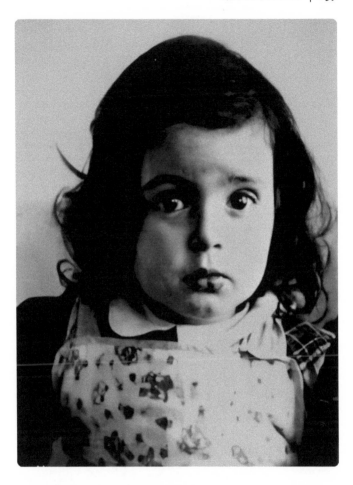

Mirjam Lewkowicz *was killed at Auschwitz at age two on September 17, 1943, along with her mother, Bettina, and six-month-old baby brother, Hugo. Her father died on June 13, 1944. Mirjam's maternal grandparents were killed on October 12, 1942, and her uncle on September 30, 1942. Little Mirjam was my grandmother's niece.*

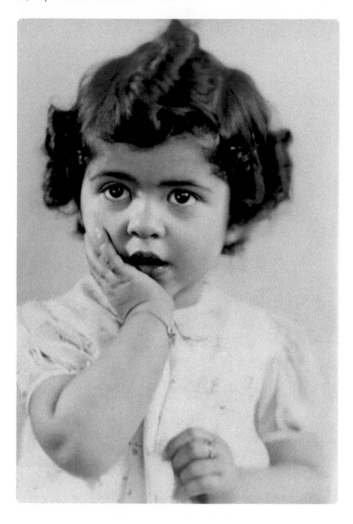

Kaatje Esther Hijman, *age two, killed at Auschwitz on November 13, 1942, along with her mother, Dora, her grandmother (also named Kaatje) and Kaatje's little seven-month-old cousin, Miriam. Kaatje's father, grandfather, aunt, and uncle all died after her. Notice the tiny ring on her finger and sweet little bracelet on her arm. Little Kaatje was also one of my grandmother's many nieces.*

Abraham Groenteman, *age two, was gassed on May 21, 1943, along with his mother, Henderina, age twenty-eight, and father, Abraham, age thirty-five. This little boy's extended family all died in the Holocaust, including his seven aunts, three uncles, numerous cousins, and both sets of grandparents. The toy car visible in this picture was my inspiration for giving the van Cleef twins wooden cars handmade by their grandfather. Abraham was one of my grandmother's many nephews.*

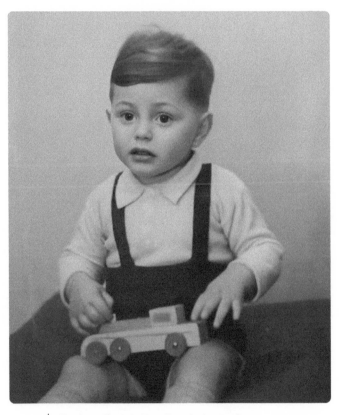

Abraham Groenteman. Born in Amsterdam, Holland on June 16, 1940. Died at the Sobibor Concentration Camp in Poland on May 21, 1943.

TRANSLATIONS

*T*he following are the more unusual Dutch first names of family members, their translations, and modern English equivalents. Dutch words and phases used in this book, along with their meanings, are also presented.

Girls' Names
> **Schoontje** / beautiful / *Belle, Linda, Bella*
> **Vroutje** / little lady / *Donna*
> **Klaartje** / clear, bright / *Clara, Claire*
> **Kaatje** / pure / *Katherine*
> **Duifje** / little dove / *Jemma, Jemima*
> **Betje** / devoted to God / *Elisabeth*
> **Frouke** / little lady / *Donna*
> **Engeltje** / angel / *Angela*
> **Matje** / gift of the Lord / *Michelle*
> **Floor** / flower / *Flora*
> **Vogeltje** / little bird / *Ava*
> **Sientje** / freedom / *Frances*

Mietje / oil of joy (myrrh) / *Miriam*
Roosje / rose / *Rose*
Zulma / healthy / *Eloise*

Boys' Names

Mordechai / warrior / *Andrew*
Levie / joined in harmony / *Lee*
Gerrit / brave with a spear / *Garret*
Gerson / exile/sojourner / *Doran/Dorian*
Elkan /
Hartog / deer / *Hartford, Henry*
Maurits / dark-skinned / *Morris*
Jechiel / God will live / *Jeffrey*

Dutch Words

- **schoonmoeder** / lovely mother / *mother-in-law*
- **lieve** / dear / *darling*
- **koffiemolen** / coffee mill / *coffee grinder*
- **kleine** / little / *small, little*
- **stukje** / piece / *a bit, a piece*
- **meisje** / *girl*
- **Tante** / *aunt*
- **Oom** / *uncle*
- **Oma** / grandmother / *Grandma*
- **Opa** / grandfather / *Grandpa*
- **jenever** / gin *(an alcoholic drink)*
- **poffertjes** / puffed cakes / *small puffy pancakes*
- **kroketten** / ground meat rolled in bread crumbs and fried/*croquettes*
- **bitterballen** / breaded meatballs / *no equivalent*
- **saucijzenbroodje** / sausage roll

- **mannetje** / little man / *kiddo*
- **lever** / liver / *liver, as in the organ*
- **razzia** / round up / *raid*
- **schatje** / sweet baby / *sweetheart*
- **stofzuiger** / stuff sucker / *vacuum cleaner*
- **moeder** / mother / *Mama*
- **koekjes** / cookies
- **Goedemorgen** / *good morning*
- **zoute dropjes** / salty licorice / *no equivalent*
- **verschrikkelijk** / *horrible, dreadful*

DUTCH PHRASES AND EXPRESSIONS

Er is meer dan een kleine Hansje in die kelder.
There is more than one Hansel in the basement.

This is an ancient Dutch phrase indicating that a woman was pregnant. The original phrase (originating from the 1600s) translates to "there is a little Hansel in the basement," singular.

It was considered improper for a woman to announce a pregnancy, so a family would have friends over, pass around a special drink and say, *"Er is een kleine Hansje in de kelder,"* and everyone would know, *wink wink,* that the lady of the house was expecting.

- **Wil je een kopje thee?** *Would you like a cup of tea?*
- **Waar ben jij?** *Where are you?*
- **Ben je helemaal gek?** *Are you completely crazy?*
- **het oude Markenpleintje** / *old Jewish market square*
- **mijn lieve schatje** / *my dearest one, my sweetheart*
- **mijn lieve zus** / *my dear sister*

- **lekkere hapjes** / *delicious bites*
- **Soep met balletjes** / *soup with balls, little dumplings*
- **slagroom tartje** / *whipped cream pastry, eclair*
- **moeder's mooiste** / *mother's most beautiful*
- **schatje boetje** / *sweetie, sweet baby*
- **pas op** / *be careful*
- **hou op** / *stop it*
- **kijk eventjes** / *take a look*
- **Gelukkig Nieuwjaar** / *Happy New Year*
- **godverdomme** / *God damn it*
- **blote billen gezicht** / *bare bum face*
- **goeie hemel** / *good heavens*
- **houd je grote bek dicht** / *keep your big mouth shut*
- **spikkeltjes kaas** / *speckled cheese (gouda cheese with caraway seeds)*
- **helemaal niet** / *completely nothing / not in the least*
- **Goede middag mevrouw.** Good afternoon miss.
- **Wat kan ik voor jou doen?** What can I do for you?

German Phrases

- **aschmutziges Jüdisches Schwein** / *filthy Jewish pig*

- **Kristaalnacht** / *night of broken glass*

- **Willst du eine Tasse Kaffee mit mir** / *Do you want a cup of coffee with me?*

- **Großdeutscher Reichstag** / *Greater German Parliament*

- **Endlösung der Judenfrage** / *Final Solution to the Jewish Question*

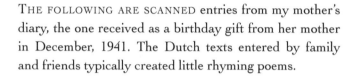

THE FOLLOWING ARE SCANNED entries from my mother's diary, the one received as a birthday gift from her mother in December, 1941. The Dutch texts entered by family and friends typically created little rhyming poems.

First entry in the diary, from her mother.
December 29, 1941

Dearest Sophia
As you go along this road, do not walk into a hedge. Keep your eyes open. Then you will not be fooled.
your Mother

~

My mother wrote her own entry in her diary:

"Today is January 29, 1941. I am fourteen years old and in the 2nd class at H.B.S. I received three Fails on my report card.

We had a lovely Christmas, although the Christmas tree is now gone. We enjoyed turkey and rabbit. I do not think the next year will be so good."

Her brief premonition would prove true—the next year, and three more after that, would be beyond anything that anyone could ever have imagined.

Translated diary entry from Mina Vittali-Tas
January 31, 1941

Dear little Sophia
A little fuss for my niece ..
Always be fresh and clean, and pay close attention at
school. Also don't forget, that you've often eaten with us.

Often you came for something, a few ribbons for your
hair. And when you were being naughty, perhaps you
thought I did not know. Always be good, then you will
never have the strap.
Your Tante Mina

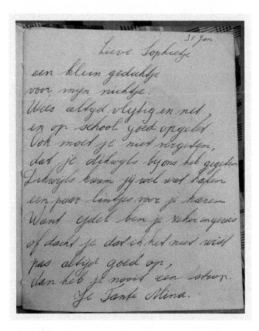

Translated diary entry from Lea de Vries-Hijman.
August 20, 1941

Dear little Sophia
If you're mad at someone, just count to ten.
This forgives much, as you will see.
Always give everyone a kind word as that pleases all.
Tante Lea

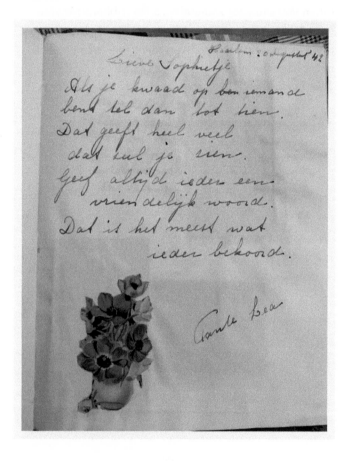

Diary entry from Duifje Coppenhagen, July 17, 1942,
two months before dying in Auschwitz.

Dear Fietje

Be as clean as the flowers of spring
Her beauty is the image of youth.
The crown that a girl should wear displays:
Simplicity, Honesty and Virtue.

Your cousin
Dolly Coppenhagen

LINKS AND REFERENCES

$\mathcal{T}$he following websites provided substantial research information and were of great assistance in ensuring historical accuracy.

Statistical Analysis of Twin Birthrates in the Netherlands
https://www.psychologytoday.com/us/blog/how-we-do-it/201707/twins-and-more-too-much-good-thing

The Netherlands - a nation starved by war
https://en.wikipedia.org/wiki/Dutch_famine_of_1944–45

Limitations on Dutch Jews: 1940 - 1944
https://www.facinghistory.org/resource-library/text/anti-jewish-measures-netherlands-and-belgium-between-1940-and-1944

Germany's Branding of the Jews; History of the Badge of the Yellow Star

https://www.yadvashem.org/odot_pdf/Microsoft%
20Word%20-%202430.pdf

Joods Monument; the Dutch Jewish Online Monument
https://www.joodsmonument.nl

"Mercy killings" in Nazi Germany
https://www.facinghistory.org/holocaust-and-human-
behavior/chapter-8/unworthy-live

United States Memorial Holocaust Museum
https://www.ushmm.org

The World Holocaust Remembrance Centre
https://www.yadvashem.org

Testing Human Bonds Within Nations: Jews in the Occupied Netherlands
http://www.jstor.org/stable/2150408

German, European & Polish Concentration Camps
https://www.jewishvirtuallibrary.org/concentration-
camps

The Gas Chambers
https://www.thoughtco.com/zyklon-b-gas-chamber-
poison-1779688

Rumanian Doctor Describes a Normal Day at Auschwitz
https://www.theguardian.com/century/1940-
1949/Story/0,127738,00.html

Looting, Theft and Expropriation in the Netherlands, WW2
https://www.jcpa.org/phas/phas-gerstens00.htm

German Seizure of Unsuspecting Citizens in Occupied Nations
https://en.wikipedia.org/wiki/Roundup_(history)

Saving the Children of Holland
https://www.timesofisrael.com/where-500-children-disappeared-from-nazi-clutches-a-new-dutch-shoah-museum-emerges/

Saving The Children: History Of The Organized Effort To Rescue Jewish Children,1942-1945
Saving the Children; amazon.com

The Hollandse Schouwburg Theatre
https://europeanmemories.net/memorial-heritage/hollandsche-schouwburg-national-holocaust-memorial/

Dutch Workers Protest Anti-Jewish Regulations
https://en.wikipedia.org/wiki/February_strike

Betraying Neighbours—the Legacy of Bounty Hunters
https://www.latimes.com/archives/la-xpm-2002-dec-01-adfg-bountyhunt1-story.html

What the World Knew - Allied Powers choose sides
https://www.independent.co.uk/news/world/world-history/holocaust-allied-forces-knew-concentration-camp-discovery-us-uk-soviets-secret-documents-a7688036.html

Establishment of the Judenrat; Jewish Councils

http://www.holocaust-
lestweforget.com/jewishcouncil.html

Malaria Epidemics in Europe, 1922 - 1930
http://www.scielo.br/scielo.php?script=sci_arttext&pid=
S0104-59702011000200009

Human Hair for Profit
https://jewishcurrents.org/january-4-human-hair/

The Mengele Twins
https://www.thoughtco.com/mengeles-children-twins-of-
auschwitz-1779486

https://candlesholocaustmuseum.org/learn/mengele-
twins.html

**Forced Sterilization of Mixed-marriage Jewish
Women**
https://www.jta.org/1943/11/24/archive/germans-
sterilizing-thousands-of-dutch-jews-hunt-for-fugitives-
continues

Canada's Role in the Liberation of the Netherlands
https://www.thecanadianencyclopedia.ca/en/article/
liberation-of-holland

https://en.wikipedia.org/wiki/
Canada–Netherlands_relations

Lewy body Dementia
https://www.alz.org/alzheimers-dementia/what-is-
dementia/types-of-dementia/lewy-body-dementia

EPILOGUE

*O*nce that secret first door into my mother's family's past fully opened to me, I could not help but walk through it, and what followed was an empathic urging to continue that journey. I needed to know.

Even after almost five years of deep genealogy diving and internet research, I continue to discover more people connected to my family, more revealed dates to reflect upon, and more lives to imagine.

After that first rush of immediate family, the next and subsequent waves of information extended to the family of family: siblings of spouses who married, had children, who married, had children. Hundreds upon hundreds of people. Each one gently added to our family tree, creating the barest semblance of a memorial, that most ancient of human ceremonies denied to them in real life.

I'm sorry. I am so, so sorry.

To date, June 2021, I have located over 1,200 Dutch relatives that died in the Holocaust. This is a sombre and incomprehensible number.

Yet I know I have not found them all. I do know that the ones still to be discovered have lives and stories tragically sharing the same themes: arrest, deportation, humiliation, destination, annihilation. Who will remember them if not us? Who will reflect on their catastrophic end if not us? My knowing has changed my attitude towards life, my worldview, how I treat others, my perception of what matters, and what endures.

Nothing I have, or will ever face in life, could remotely compare with what my family suffered, what their neighbours and friends suffered, what millions of others suffered, all through no fault of their own. They were guilty of nothing. I have a deep connection to this suffering; it gives me an inner strength to persevere, no matter what.

Beyond the unfolding of vast amounts of uncovered genealogical data appeared stark historical realities; sobering crumbs of daily life at war deemed too insignificant to enter the mainstream world of textbooks and essays. I did not know, for example, that Jewish people were forbidden to even walk on the sunny side of a street.

What sort of human mind consciously concocts such ridiculous restrictions—put into action with a gleeful rubbing of hands, a delighted chortling—for no other purpose than to subvert and destroy another human.

Random thoughts of my ancestral family are with me every day. Life's routines: cooking, working, shopping, birthdays, holidays—anything and everything. I imagine how it was for them and how easy it is for me. Most of all,

I remember them when I look into the faces of my children and grandchildren.

Another place, another time. It could have been all of us.

My hope is that the world has not become dull and immune to yet another Holocaust story. True, the world has given its pity, bestowed due respect and honour—the receiving of which sincerely acknowledged and humbly appreciated by its recipients.

But there is a concerning possibility. As witnessing the same violent scene reenacted multiple times causes it to lose its ferocity, pushing the Holocaust in people's faces yet again carries the risk of it glazing them over until its importance and message is no longer seen. As a scab grows overs a wound, the skin underneath becomes devoid of sensation.

To me, this is a multi-faceted, precious story. If I don't treasure it, record it, and share it, I will have squandered it. All those hundreds of dates—the dashes between them silently waiting for a voice to speak on their behalf.

Each new generation owns the right to truth. Those who know have an obligation to tell, and the knowing of it catalyzes change. The telling must be a welcome action free from oppression, prejudice, subversion, fear or shame.

Perhaps there are more twins waiting to be discovered.

Or better still …

waiting to be born.

BLURRING THE LINES

This book intentionally blurs the lines between historical fiction, non-fiction, memoir and biography.

I am indebted to those friends and professionals who assisted me so generously with this manuscript, and gave so much of their time, expertise, suggestions, and empathy. Interestingly, each one asked which stories were fiction and which facts were true (other than the obvious facts cited and documented).

The following specific "bits" from the individual short stories are based on true events and are exact in their details. Those listed below are events or items that I was specifically asked about as to whether they were true or fictionalized:

- Schoontje Wijnschenk's triplets. Yes, she did give birth to triplets over a three days in July, 1840, and yes, she herself was an only child.
- The Wijnschenk's family infant deaths. This family had thirteen children in total. Two boys

did not survive infancy, as well as a little girl, born after the triplets, who died at age two.

- Flora, Duifje and Sophia did indeed all live within a fifteen minute walk of each other.
- Duifje and my mother did have identical haircuts and hair colour.
- Christina Vittali's fiancée, who was a locally famous opera singer, never returned home.
- Christina Vittali kept a war diary almost daily for the entire duration of the war; I have these in my possession.
- The deserted, looted house adjoined to Mina Vittali's is described exactly as I observed it in 1978.
- My mother's tall, bottom-chafing bicycle with no tires left , only rims, was indeed the one she had during the war. She even brought this bicycle with her to Canada when she immigrated and I have ridden it.
- My grandfather did give my mother an itchy, heavy coil of dirty construction rope to trade for food out in the country.
- That doomed rooster in a sack was most definitely real!
- There were three sets of twins born to relatives all in one year (1928), and these relatives all lived in close proximity to each other. Additionally, the Bril twins did live only three minutes away as well.
- Diamonds in liver. My mother told me how people would hide valuables in paper packages with "liver" written across the front.
- Little Samuel Wennek was indeed too small to see over the policeman's desk. He remembers

standing on tip-toe to try and see the officer who was speaking to him.

- Samuel recalls vividly watching his grandparents being shoved into the back of a truck, and remembers them waving goodbye as they were being driven away.
- Every first and last name used throughout this book are the actual names of relatives who truly did live in whatever time and place I wrote them into.
- The Vittali family (along with many others) were reduced to eating tulip bulbs, along with beets, beets and more beets in the winter of 1945 (sugar beets, not garden vegetable beets). My Uncle Joe declared that after the war, he could never eat beets again.
- And lastly, yes, I have planted tulips halfway across Canada, and quite a few apple trees as well!